LIVING FORWARD, GIVING BACK

Living Forward, Giving Back

A Practical Guide to Fulfillment in Midlife and Beyond

Isabelle St-Jean

Inspired Momentum
Suite 413 – 651 Moberly Road
Vancouver, British Columbia
Canada V5Z 4B2
www.inspiredmomentum.com
info@inspiredmomentum.com

Layout and design: Julie Cochrane
Cover concept: Isabelle St-Jean
Cover design: Peggy Cady, Lara Shecter
Cover photos: Janet Rerecich
Cover models: Greg Bennett and Rebecca Davies
Editing: Naomi Pauls
Proofreading: Anita Flegg

Permission for the poem "Love after Love" by Derek Walcott granted by Farrar, Straus and Giroux, LLC
Permission for the poem "Snowflakes" granted by Larry Robinson

Library and Archives Canada Cataloguing in Publication

St-Jean, Isabelle, 1955–
   Living forward, giving back: a practical guide to fulfillment in midlife and beyond / Isabelle St-Jean; editor, Naomi Pauls.

ISBN 978-0-9780319-2-3

   1. Middle-aged persons—Conduct of life. 2. Middle age.
3. Self-realization. 4. Retirement. I. Pauls, Naomi II. Title.

BF724.6.S23 2008   158.1084'4   C2008-906415-1

Printed in Canada by Friesens

For my children, Misha and Natasha,
my Balinese friends Sang Tu and Plentung,
and all those helping to bring about
a brighter future

Contents

PREFACE AND ACKNOWLEDGMENTS

At least a couple of years before baby boomers became a regular topic in the media, I began to wonder what had happened to the collective identity and spirit of our generation. The flower power of the early seventies seemed to have wilted, I thought. Yet even as our generation was blamed for having become greedy and selfish, I sensed that below the ground of our daily pre-occupations, something else was about to burst forth among us.

The calling for this book came as a desire to explore, to understand and articulate the deeper questions, motives and aspirations stirring in our midst. During interviews and research, I quickly saw that our generation is char-acterized by diversity but that several themes still connect us. I observed that many of us, like me, are feeling that midlife restlessness and yearning to in-vest some of our time and energy in making a difference. And I saw that those approaching or entering retirement are seeking a new way to re-engage in a purposeful and balanced way of life. Perfect timing! Just when our Mother Earth and its people are in dire need of caring attention and focused actions, we are about to have more time and resources than any other gen-eration in the past.

This book features examples of men and women who have sustained or retrieved the heartfelt values and ideals of their youth. Now grounded in spiritual maturity, these people have been better able to take effective, joy-ful and loving actions toward the betterment of our world. Inspired by the courage and the fiery energy burning in the human spirit, I aim to help you, through this book, to reignite your own spark of creative and meaningful purpose.

While writing, I not only listened to others intently, but also had to lis-ten in stillness and silence as never before to tap my inner guidance. This is not a book of ready-made answers or linear instructions for midlife and beyond. Given my deep respect for the wisdom innate in the soul, I am not attempting to nudge you toward simplistic solutions, nor am I offering a seemingly clever formula to override your inner knowing. While you read this, set aside your questions about what you are to *do* and let the stories speak to your heart about ways to *be*; it is in the process of embodying our highest values that we realize ways to turn them into daily actions and positive results.

Let these pages inspire you and validate some of your deepest feelings. And at the end, the summary will help affirm your own best answers while you may choose to integrate some of the suggested practices into your life. From my learning and experience through three decades in the field of human potential development, these are practices I believe can lead to true, joyful fulfillment at this time on Earth.

During the three years it has taken to complete this book, I have felt such gratitude for the support and help I received from relatives, friends and colleagues, too many to name here. My teenage children, Misha and particularly Natasha, have been encouraging me as they looked forward to attending my book launch. I have a special indebtedness to my editor, Naomi Pauls, who graciously and patiently helped me to distil the essential messages from my first few wordy drafts. I also thank my designers, Peggy Cady, Lara Shecter and Julie Cochrane, the photographer Janet Rerecich, and the models for the cover photo, Greg Bennett and Rebecca Davies. Lastly, I feel an immense thankfulness toward all of those who have entrusted me with their candid stories and allowed me to share them with you.

INTRODUCTION

I will always remember the summer evening when Greg and Rebecca came to the Vancouver shoreline to be photographed gazing over the lumines-cent horizon. While they enjoyed a moment of contemplation, I looked at them and at the golden sky. Across Burrard Inlet, the coastal mountains in the distance, wearing different shades of blue, reminded me of the diversity among us all as I stood, filled with anticipation about my writing journey. Meanwhile, Janet captured the images now embracing the pages you are about to read.

Do you recall when, like Greg, you last sat in nature and reflected on your life's path? Perhaps it has been a while since, like Rebecca, you stood facing the water, wondering what you are called to be or to do now or in the next few years. And what about our planet and the humanity it carries; what does it ask of us now? Can you hear it?

Living forward, the first part of this book's title, is not about attempting to bypass the present, nor is it about living in the future. The *now* and its wondrous possibilities remain the ground of our current reality and of our state of being. Living forward means that in the spirit of our interconnected-ness, we embrace a creative orientation, knowing that we each have the ca-pacity to shape our life and to collectively bring about a better future. And living forward means that we are mindful of our responsibilities to the Earth and its people, because we are the ancestors of our children and of the gen-erations yet to come.

Giving back is not just about philanthropy or volunteering; it is also about contributing our truth, our wisdom, our talents and our passions in intentional and meaningful ways. Giving back, for boomers particularly, means that we are grateful for the opportunities and resources we have been given; from that gratitude comes an outflow of thankfulness in action.

This book is meant for you especially if you were born in the midpoint decades of the past century, between 1946 and 1964. By now, the eldest in this generation are entering the gateway of eldership. Others are traversing the exciting terrain of their sixth decade; yet others are moving through their forties, soon to face the most significant questions of their life. Based on my research, studies and my own personal and professional experience, this book offers my insights into the patterns, the trends and the commonality that characterize the journey of our diverse generation.

Like me, you are probably aware that we are at a crossroads in time. A time when we are all summoned to be and do what is needed for our world to become more socially and economically just, more loving and more sustainable. Clearly, we have already engaged in this complex and treacherous undertaking and it is building momentum, an inspired momentum, I would say. Numerous examples of people contributing to this great turning are included in these pages.

The first section addresses the collectivity of our generation as a whole. Chapter 2 takes you back to retrieve what we have inherited from some of our past visionary leaders. Their legacy is still with us, reverberating in our collective consciousness. And our inheritance from them is prompting us to build on the foundational and timeless truths embodied by their words and actions.

As you set foot on the inner landscape of midlife in the second section, you will be encouraged to replace the perception of this passage as a crisis with the idea of it being an exciting opportunity. To navigate it well, each of us needs introspection to tap the infinite source of guidance and life energy available within. As the psychologist Erik Erikson stated many years ago, midlife is characterized by the call of generativity: an expansive desire to care not only for ourselves and our loved ones but also by participating in the betterment of society.

Typically, as we traverse the midlife passage, we experience this "fire in the belly" urging us to show up, to liberate our greatness and to open with more audacity into the fullness of life. But after years of laboring in a workplace culture that may be incongruent with your values and deeper needs, you may need to excavate your authentic self. That inner self helps you tap new energies and retrieve your passions as you leave behind your professional life or reorient your work life. The stories in this section shed light on some obstacles and illuminate possibilities while stimulating your generosity of spirit.

The third section explores the changing territory of "re-engagement," still formally called retirement. This life transition can be a portal to vital new engagements, as you will see through the stories in these chapters. In this portal you will naturally be drawn to reassess your lifestyle and reaffirm the innermost values from which your renewed purpose and well-being will flourish. The questions at the end of each chapter throughout the book are meant to sharpen your awareness and generate insights while you approach or move through your own transitions and re-engagement process.

The final section explores some of the factors and dynamics that hinder or support us as we endeavor to bring about the world we so want. One chapter celebrates the timely contributions of women who are stepping forward in unprecedented numbers to lead and to take powerful, caring actions. In these pages, you will also read how women differ from men when involved in philanthropic pursuits.

The closing chapter explains what it means to *lead*, not just *leave*, a legacy in your personal and your professional life. Herein is a reminder that every thought and action has a powerful ripple effect. Furthermore, when you begin to see your life as a gift entrusted unto you, a sense of mission will naturally arise and guide you. As you uncover your next road map, your True North will point to your own balance of joyful, restorative and participatory activities in the relational community to which you belong. The last chapter also includes an integrative summary with practices that can support your creative orientation, foster your longevity, and generate numerous moments of serenity and happiness.

A Generation
at the Crossroads

CHAPTER 1

Challenges and Possibilities

Sometimes it falls upon a generation to be great.
You can be that generation.

—Nelson Mandela

History reveals that this generation, born out of peace, has been the most influential in our human evolution. In the past few years in particular, a collective turning toward life-affirming values has given rise to new initiatives, actions and positive change. Although we are all touched by the momentum of this movement, as individuals we respond or actively participate in different ways.

Looking back, even the circumstances of our birth, in the aftermath of a major war, predisposed us to become a crusader generation, agents of peace and change. "Make Love, Not War!" we chanted through the sixties and seventies. You may have engaged in some form of activism, perhaps marched on the streets for peace, feeling part of a collective identity fueled by shared convictions. Together, we united in a vigorous, concerted movement to stand up for peace and to protest against other issues that mattered. We made the Vietnam War politically untenable.

The following account of marching for peace and experiencing a profound commonality may trigger your own recollections of what that was like. In his book *How Can I Help?*, Ram Dass, the former Harvard psychology professor formerly known as Richard Alpert, recalls being involved in the largest demonstration in American history. It was in June 1982: the antinuclear demonstration in New York City. With fond memories of the march, Ram Dass states that because there were so many people crowded on the side streets waiting to join the main route, it took four hours for the march to get moving. His book describes this moment of history-making:

> It became very clear, very early on, that the whole thing had a life of its own. . . . What was most extraordinary, however, was the way in which people stayed in place right where they were. For four hours. People seemed to understand that the way we were standing our ground—in place, in peace—was as much a statement as the march itself, maybe more. It was the way we were being. The power and potential of that was tangible. Everyone felt it. Having felt it, it was not anything you were likely to forget.

Memories of such events bring up nostalgia in me, perhaps because I have had fewer opportunities in the past decade or two to experience a collective field of such magnitude and unified purpose. The phenomenon of gathering together in great numbers for a cause seems to have lost some of its momentum in the West since the eighties. Of course, with our widespread use of the Internet, we can now stay in communication and reach a much greater number of people in our networking and activism. For example, online petitions are increasingly popular, effectively pressuring the governments involved. Although it is evidently practical to use technology to reach a large number of people, the exercise of signing a petition in front of one's computer does not duplicate the powerful spirit of unity Ram Dass referred to in the excerpt above. After the eighties, into the nineties, our sense of collective identity seemed to dissipate as our generation scattered in various directions.

Divergent values across the decades

Although the boomers were a relatively homogeneous mass with respect to their ideals during their youth, over time, they were influenced and motivated by a host of different factors, circumstances and aspirations. Looking across the diversity of our generation now, one can observe that some of those who marched passionately for peace a few decades ago have only deepened their engagements in humanitarian and/or ecological concerns. They are part of a growing segment of the population described by Paul Ray and Sherry Ruth Anderson in their book *The Cultural Creatives*, written in the year 2000. This book, backed by more than ten years of research, identified three major groups of citizens according to their shared ideologies: the Moderns, the Traditionals and the Cultural Creatives.

Perhaps you yourself identify with the Cultural Creatives, who hold values such as the preservation of nature, relationships, helping others, spirituality, and being proactive and optimistic. Like many others in this subculture, I have shaped my life's work from such heartfelt values. For some of us, however, "compassionate fatigue" may have set in as we've watched our efforts eroded or opposed by lack of political will, the consumer-driven machine or the intangible forces of the status quo. Since our youthful years, our ardent desire to activate social change has somewhat subsided while we have experienced, at the same time, a conspicuous absence of inspired political leadership.

According to Ray and Anderson, the Traditionals tend to adopt values such as patriarchy, religious teachings like the Bible as the primary source of guidance, traditional gender roles, and repression of immoral behavior. At the end of the twentieth century, the Traditionals were estimated to represent approximately 25 percent of the population in the United States, some of them belonging to the boomer generation. Some Traditionals are also developing an awareness of environmental issues, as they seek to leave a better world for their progeny.

Among the third group, the Moderns, some may have embraced humanistic values in their idealistic youth. But over time their ideals faded behind the pragmatic preoccupations of daily living, and they became increasingly competitive, techno-driven and consumed by their fast-paced life. If you are among this group, you may have at times felt caught in the complex matrix of factors and pressures that accompany the mainstream "success" mindset, characterized by a focus on status, comfort and material wealth. Ray and Anderson estimated that the Moderns, likely spanning two or three generations, amounted to 48 percent of the U.S. population by the end of the nineties.

Of course, if we look into the personal history of any one member of these three groups, we find a variety of inner and outer forces influencing that person's particular set of values and behaviors. Recently, one of my midlife coaching clients who oriented his early career choices toward money-making and status explained that as a child he had suffered greatly from his parents' lack of financial means. When he looked for a sense of direction in his early twenties, he was persuaded by others to seek a career in which he was virtually assured to achieve status and wealth. With his hard work and perseverance he became a successful lawyer in his community, but at the cost of his personal fulfillment. In chapter 5, "The Homecoming Journey," you can read more about this man's midlife realizations. As this story shows, without proactively choosing the values we want to live by, we often become overly influenced by societal pressures.

Regardless of what group we identify with, many of us have become stressed and perhaps even exhausted while trying to "get ahead" or simply maintain a certain standard of living. The prevalence of consumerism really hits home when we consider some of the new trends in the United States. In certain affluent neighborhoods some people purchase a secondary home for the sole purpose of storing the excess stuff that the primary home can no longer contain. All around us, the media has been contributing to this trend toward rampant consumerism.

In Canada, a 2007 survey reported in *Maclean's* magazine revealed that 70 percent of adults watch one to four hours of television daily. A young man working for Amnesty International recently shared with me some of his observations about his midlife parents. "They watch so much TV," he said, "and they think that what they see there is the real world." Through decades of marketing efforts, corporate America and the mainstream media have been feeding the narcissistic tendencies of some boomers. Additionally, the marketing industry and its incessant promotion of consumerism have created what Allen Kanner and Mary Gomes call the "false consumer self." In a chapter entitled "The All-Consuming Self" in the book *Ecopsychology*, the authors explain that advertising not only distorts the truth but actually lies. As advertisers project the image of blissful consumers in numerous commercials, the "false consumer self" unconsciously associates those products with happiness. In chapter 9, which includes lifestyle choices, I have more to say about the false consumer self and the alternative trend toward simplifying one's life and consuming less.

Shadows and light at home

In addition to the pressures of "keeping up with the Joneses" that some among us feel, stressors are mounting at home as the rising divorce rate indicates. In the middle years, few marriages are actually thriving and providing fulfillment to the partners. Too often, the accumulation of distancing behaviors and unresolved wounds makes the relationship cave in and break down. Although some couples maintain a seemingly adequate marital life, most struggle to break through ingrained dysfunctional patterns of relating. Chapter 7, on relationships, explores this part of our lives in much more depth.

In addition to the challenges we have in our primary relationships, our children and teens are increasingly at risk of feeling alienated by the pervasive erosion of family-oriented values and the speed of modern life. In the absence of consistent and loving guidance from their parents, teenagers more readily absorb negative messages from their televisions, their computers and their peers. Tragically, such teens can become unmotivated and are at risk of drifting toward whatever negative influence they may encounter. On the other hand, in homes where they are provided a truly caring environment, some of today's teens are astonishingly insightful and motivated to be of service to humanity and/or environmental issues.

Another positive trend in the realm of relationships is for men and women to become involved in midlife and enter a new marriage based on common values and shared purpose. Being together in compelling endeavors, these couples find the synergy emerging between them to be energizing, joyful and satisfying. You will read about such wonderful unions in chapter 7.

Facing the challenges

Considered to be the most affluent in human history, the boomers' generation has generally achieved financial success. Having satisfied our basic needs for shelter, sustenance and safety, we are able to move toward higher preoccupations on Maslow's hierarchy of needs. In the past decades especially, many of us have devoted time and resources to developing our awareness, shedding limiting beliefs and evolving our consciousness. Now we want to engage that consciousness more widely in our social and environmental spheres.

Yet being conscious and present to the looming dangers of our times can be difficult to tolerate. Often it is just too painful to hear more about the depletion of our natural resources, the threats of global warming, the starvation of people in the poorest countries, the extinction of animal species, and so on. Feeling overwhelmed, helpless or in despair about it all is a common reaction. Some of us try to protect ourselves from the crisis by retreating into a "comfort zone" of denial. In this zone, we may collude with others to maintain the illusion that we are safe, in control and happy.

Such collusion is more difficult to maintain now at the eleventh hour, when we are all confronted with the "inconvenient truth" so effectively demonstrated by Al Gore. As horrendous as are the threats of greater ecological disasters, another threat is even more significant. In the words of ecophilosopher and activist Joanna Macy, "The deadening of our hearts and minds is an even greater threat than global warming." This poignant statement found resonance in me when I heard Joanna speak in the San Francisco area in the fall of 2006. Like her, I believe that we must turn to one another as we acknowledge our grief for the current crisis on Earth. Paradoxically, to the extent that we can meet that grief with an open heart, humility and compassion, we can also mobilize new energies and resourcefulness to effect the needed changes.

Bringing light over the horizon, emerging trends and developments are empowering us as we traverse this difficult passage in our human evolution. Here are six of these timely changes that help us to stay oriented toward achieving the breakthrough required to meet the urgencies of our times.

Positive shifts emerging

Among the majority of us in midlife who are still involved in the workplace, there is an awakening to new ways of working and making profits. Respect for the triple bottom line is increasingly taking hold, supporting social responsibilities and sustainable practices as part of the mission, vision and daily actions of a growing number of corporations. Corporate philanthropy is also a newer trend, in recognition of the importance of giving back to community. There is a systemic, collective impetus to find new ways to work that better serve the needs of communities near and far while preventing further harm to nature.

On the personal as well as the corporate level, many of us are addressing larger questions such as this: how do we work and prosper in harmony and integrity while bringing about the socially and ecologically sustainable world we urgently need? This question is at the core of the anthology project I initiated and co-edited with Dawson Church and his team at Elite Books. In *Einstein's Business: Engaging Soul, Imagination and Excellence in the Workplace*, fifty authors share their ideas, visions and practical tools as they answer important and timely questions. Margaret Wheatley, one of the contributing authors, is an internationally renowned speaker and consultant. One of her simplest yet most powerful calls to action is for us to "turn to one another."

Turning to one another is part of a second positive trend, which has developed particularly over the past decade. It exemplifies a new kind of thinking that fosters communication and collaboration through various forms of actions and conversations. Numerous forms of conversations and dialogue have been created to tap our collective intelligence and augment our creative potential to bring about new ideas and practical solutions. This phenomenon is reflected on the Internet site Meetup.com. As of July 2008, there were nearly 50,000 Meetup groups around the world connecting people, in person, around more than 3,000 interests, including health, spirituality, parenting, entrepreneurship, sports and education. And in our hunger to connect with others, we are beginning to melt the barriers of genders and generations as never before.

For example, in some conferences normally attended mostly by middle-aged people, youth delegations are increasingly welcomed to be part of the overall conversation. I participated in one such event organized by the Society for Organizational Learning in the spring of 2007 in Atlanta, Georgia. There I observed boomers amazed at the freshness of insights emanating from the young, and the youth pleasantly surprised by the supportive appreciation of their elders. This trend toward more open dialogues and conversations helps us to counteract the risk of feeling isolated following our countless hours spent solo behind our computers.

Among the crucial conversations occurring, some generate organizations and projects devoted to serving humanity and the natural world. This third trend, of an increasing number of groups dedicated to social issues and the environment, is acknowledged and celebrated in the book *Blessed Unrest*, by Paul Hawken. In this book Hawken shows convincingly that a movement of people from several generations has been gathering momentum, especially since the dawn of this new century. In a multitude of non-profit organizations, people are finding ways to take actions fueled by their passions and shared visions. In their collective efforts, they embrace life-affirming values such as social justice, compassion in action, and reverence for nature.

A fourth development has arisen from the passage of time across our generation. Generativity, the inner force that causes a "fire in the belly" in midlife, is a resource that is being harnessed in many ways. In part, this energy is expressed through an unprecedented involvement by those in midlife in benevolent projects, mentoring hours, community volunteering, and so on. Awareness of our own mortality begins to hit home at this time of life, thus we become more and more preoccupied with making a difference in others' lives. This timely stage in our development brims with potential for generous acts and loving energy available for us to tap. The following chapters feature examples of people who have made great use of this inner force. Chapter 4, in particular, discusses research into the benefits of giving.

The fifth emerging trend is that in midlife, creativity awakens anew because we feel compelled to reclaim our authentic selves. As we reconnect with this part of ourselves, often forgotten beneath the layers of roles we have played, we ache to find new forms of expression. Among my coaching clients, friends and others I have interviewed, creative urges are showing up and finding expression through a variety of satisfying endeavors. With re-awakened desires such as wanting to write, sing or lead in some way, we yearn to rediscover ourselves, to free our voices and to liberate our creative genius. Although I never stopped being creative in various ways in my life, I recently returned, after more than thirty years, to the art of painting with soft pastels. I am astonished at the pleasure I felt while freeing myself into exuberance and completing a large, wildly-colored flower, now adorning a wall in my home.

Not only does this creative surge provide new possibilities for innovation,

CHALLENGES AND POSSIBILITIES | 11

it also serves to re-enchant our world with the products of our self-expression. In our daily lives, tapping our creativity helps us to re-source ourselves, reawaken our passions and find a much-needed sense of balance. And given that our mainstream culture tends to lean heavily toward extreme pragmatism, creativity is important to restore our relationship with the awesome resource within that is our imagination. You may recall Albert Einstein's quotation asserting that "imagination is more important than knowledge." Clearly, our capacity to imagine and create is the doorway to sustainable visions that we must continue to realize through our actions. In the spirit of creativity, I urge you to follow this call to action I heard from an unknown source: *"Dare to walk your creative genius down the wildest unknown ways."*

The sixth positive trend is that as we enter eldership, currently called the senior years, we will remain actively engaged in society. The old paradigms of "retirement," which used to be a synonym for a life of leisure, are giving way to new models of a balanced life that includes vital and purposeful engagement. Given our longer life expectancy, more people are staying in the workplace for additional years or even decades. A new flexibility is emerging, allowing elders to continue contributing their knowledge and talents while spending fewer hours at work, enabling them to reduce their stress and get involved in fulfilling endeavors.

From a bird's-eye view, these new trends and shifts suggest that we are beginning to link arms, across generations and across socio-economic strata. As we do so, we are intensifying our collective power and advancing the possibility of creating a breakthrough large enough to counter the risks of a global breakdown. The section entitled "The Dawning of a New World," contains both inspirational and practical ideas about our collective process of bringing forth our most desirable future.

> *Another world is not only possible, she is on her way.*
> *On a quiet day, I can hear her breathing.*
> — ARUNDHATI ROY

Like author and activist Arundhati Roy, I prefer to think of the better future we long for as an entity, a being that our actions and sustained yearnings help to become real. For that reason, I will henceforth refer to that particular kind of future as the Future (with a capital F).

While we intend to create a better Future that will be hospitable to the generations to come, we are wise to connect with those in the past who forged the way. The next chapter invites you to further integrate into your own life, in your own way, the timeless, universal truths of visionary leaders who were part of our lives in the twentieth century. As you revisit with me the legacies of these soul ancestors to our generation, I hope you will be inspired to deepen your engagement by participating in the positive turning. Together we can stand on behalf of the Future while we navigate with passion through our middle years and beyond.

Question to ponder collectively

- What does the better Future demand from each and every one of us right now?

CHAPTER 2

The Legacy of Past Visionary Leaders

*Memories of our lives, of our works
and our deeds will continue in others.*

—Rosa Parks

When I started this writing project, I was irresistibly drawn toward nature as a place that yields the tranquility conducive to deeper insights. I craved the sight of infinity and found a place to write for a few days at the highest point on a nearby island in the Pacific Northwest. There I sat, in my light-filled room with my laptop, enjoying the sight of an occasional deer family passing by. While I read a biography of Martin Luther King Jr., I suddenly realized in amazement that the day of my arrival corresponded with the fiftieth anniversary of Rosa Parks' act of courage on the bus in Montgomery, Alabama: December 1, 1955. I was awed by this coincidence and concluded that I was being supported in this work by the spirit of Rosa Parks.

In her refusal to give up her seat to a Caucasian man, Rosa Parks was no longer participating in the oppressive belief system that African-American people were inferior to Caucasian people. Paradoxically, by staying seated, she stood up for the truth that had become impossible to ignore, that freedom and dignity is the birthright of all people, regardless of race.

Reflecting on my own journey of integrity and truth-telling, I recall an incident that led to my first defining moment, at six years of age. The principal of my school had come to the classroom to talk to the students. After speaking briefly, she asked the students if they were enjoying coming to school and if so, to stand up. Gradually, all of my classmates rose, and I was the only one who stayed seated. In chapter 5, while you may explore your own significant moments, I explain why this experience at school had such an impact on me. In retrospect, it set my course in striving to lead a courageous and truthful life. Most of us are challenged to live in complete alignment with our truth, hence we yearn for leaders who can be models of integrity and congruence.

Searching for true leaders

In the past few years, I have heard a recurring question posed by many, in lamenting tones: "Just where *are* the real leaders now?" Why is there no major leader with the depth of character, truthfulness and resolve we associate with people such as Martin Luther King Jr.? In midlife especially, we long for models of authentic leadership: leaders who convey an inspired vision through their words and actions.

In the final stage of writing this book, I heard that Barack Obama had made an outstanding speech in Berlin before a crowd the size of which had not been seen since the wall was taken down in Germany. Could it be that our yearning for visionary leadership is about to be fulfilled? At this exciting time, we are seeing the resurgence of universal truths that can link us together in convergence toward the Future that wants to come through us. The past leaders' messages I am bringing forward here were witnessed by our generation in the prime of our youth. These messages can yield new harvests from the field of our collective unconscious, where seeds were planted for germination during the past century.

In a special feature on King published by *Time* magazine, in January 2006, Marian Wright Edelman, a past close associate of King and current president of the Children's Defense Fund, said:

Everybody is looking for Dr. King to come back. . . . Dr. King's vision was clear; the voice was clear. That clarity was a great loss. While we're all looking for the heroes of the '60s, a strong foundation has been laid. It spawned the next phase in taking our nation where it needs to go. Now the task is to honor them in our deeds. His words are still the framework. Where is the voice today? We're it. We've got to make the leaders hear it. He did his part. Now we need to do ours.

As Edelman stated, it is up to us, including new leaders arising such as Obama, to continue the work that Martin Luther King Jr. started. Let us revisit some of the enlightened words and ideas of extraordinary human beings from various spheres of endeavor, including science, music, spirituality and the pursuit of human rights. These include Martin Luther King Jr., John Lennon, Albert Einstein and Mother Teresa. Each in their own way has spoken about what it means to be committed, to realize the interconnectedness of all beings and to count on the power of love.

The messages of Martin Luther King Jr.

> *An individual has not started living until he can*
> *rise above the narrow confines of his individualistic*
> *concerns to the broader concerns of all humanity.*
> — MARTIN LUTHER KING JR.

In this quotation, King reminds us that taking a stand, speaking and acting on behalf of what matters most keeps us vibrantly alive. You might recall that a few days after Rosa Parks' act of courage, on December 5, 1955, Martin Luther King Jr. led his people in a boycott of bus transportation. He supported them through the hardship of walking, sometimes for miles, to get to work every day. Even as some of the walkers were subjected to numerous incidents of violence, King called on his people to practice nonviolence and to "walk and talk in the manner of love." Then, nearly a year after its start, the boycott ended in a magnificent breakthrough enabling African-Americans to claim some of their freedom and dignity: in 1956 the Supreme Court ruled that bus segregation was illegal.

With his outstanding ability to address important issues, King is known to have made powerful speeches that had timeless qualities, hence their startling relevance for our times. In one of his speeches, during the late fifties, he stated: "First, we are challenged to rise above the narrow confines of our individualistic concerns to the broader concerns of all of humanity. The new world is a world of geographical togetherness . . . brought about largely by man's scientific and technological genius." And when he said, "We have before us a glorious opportunity to inject a new dimension of love into the veins of our civilization," he explained that he was talking about the love we call agape. This is an unconditional love that lies in the essence of the human heart, and when we commit to live by heart-centered values, we can better extend that kind of love to others.

King also reminded his listeners of the responsibilities that accompany this new age and he cautioned them on the need to develop intelligent, courageous and dedicated leadership. "The urgency of the hour calls for leaders of wise judgment and sound integrity—leaders not in love with money, but in love with justice; leaders not in love with publicity, but in love with humanity; leaders who can subject their particular ego to the greatness of the cause."

Another one of King's timeless messages is that when we are no longer attached to differentiating ourselves from others, our lives are transformed. Compassion is a natural outcome of giving up the idea of who we think we are to experience our interconnection to others in the transcendent reality of oneness. Moreover, King urged the Western world to move beyond dualistic thinking and into forgiveness as well as unconditional love. The continuing crisis in the Middle East is a devastating example of minds trapped in an endless cycle of winning versus losing, victimization versus retaliation. Among those who echo King's message today, Archbishop Desmond Tutu also speaks of forgiveness as a necessary part of the equation in attempting to orchestrate our continuity on Earth.

When I met Desmond Tutu at the two Quest for Global Healing conferences I attended in Bali in December 2004 and May 2006, I was amazed by his lightness of being, graciousness and humility. There, he spoke about his book *No Future without Forgiveness*, stating that many people mistakenly think forgiveness is a passive kind of giving up and forgetting the wrong-doing of another. Desmond Tutu sees forgiveness as an act of courage based on a recognition that we are each responsible for our actions and that a process of reparation and restitution should follow wrongdoing. Forgiveness is a way of releasing the harmful anger and resentment that lodge at the gates of our heart and prevent it from opening to ourselves and to others.

Consider the following example, in which the action of a Palestinian man conveys what it means to fully embrace the spirit of forgiveness. In 2005, it was reported that the twelve-year-old son of a Palestinian man named Ismail Khatib had been killed accidentally by an Israeli soldier. The boy was holding a toy rifle that was mistakenly perceived as a real weapon by troops, who shot him during a raid. In the midst of his agonizing grief, Khatib decided to donate six of his son's organs to an Israeli hospital. When interviewed by the press, he said that he felt very good about his son's organs helping others, regardless of their nationality. Khatib hoped that through this gesture, his son's spirit would "enter the heart of every Israeli." This is a profound example of forgiveness and true greatness. It demonstrates Khatib's ability to embrace agape and unleash it into action.

This story reflects what Martin Luther King Jr. wanted us to strive for in our daily lives: to rise up to the best and most ethical way of being in the spirit of interdependence. His most powerful message can be boiled down to this, in his words: "all life is interrelated. We are all caught in an inescapable network of mutuality, tied in a single garment of destiny. Whatever affects one directly, affects all indirectly." To realize this in our innermost selves engenders a profound sense of responsibility for our fellow human beings in our "network of mutuality."

John Lennon's timeless messages

If someone thinks that love and peace is a cliché that must have been left behind in the sixties, that's his problem. Love and peace are eternal.
— JOHN LENNON

John Lennon is now a cherished memory in the minds of all boomers. In the last years of his career he really stepped forward to make a statement about what he thought matters most. You may recall the bed-in he did with Yoko Ono. It was at the Queen Elizabeth Hotel in Montreal, in 1972, that the couple stated their message in a most unusual way about peace and love. In that place inundated with media, John and Yoko were pointing us toward our highest aspirations and urging us to never let these priorities out of our sight.

Lennon stimulated our longing to live in peaceful and loving ways. He was also acutely aware of his own challenges while trying to fully embrace these values. He openly admitted that he had on occasion used violence when he felt caught in the grip of an intense conflict. Lennon recognized that we all struggle at various times with opposing forces arising from our divine nature and from our immature, not-yet-capable-of-loving smaller self. Part of what was endearing about him were his contrary ways of being, which could range from flippant, impatient and arrogant to being at peace, serene and loving. We identified with Lennon's pain and struggles, and we were moved by the inspired visions he channeled into some of his songs.

About the sixties he once said: "Now, in the sixties we were naïve, like children." Lennon claimed that his generation behaved like spoiled teenagers, indignant about not having been given the happy world they wanted. He said, "The thing the sixties did was show us the possibilities and the responsibility that we all had. It wasn't the answer. It just gave us a glimpse of the possibility." As he also suggested, the fervor of the sixties can be seen as the foreshadowing of a higher, more purposeful Future seeking to emerge through us.

Lennon certainly ignited the flame of new possibilities through his song "Imagine," created in the late seventies. By inviting us to envision a world not bound by the frontiers of countries or religions, he felt that we would be more likely to realize we had "nothing to kill or die for." He called on us to imagine a world without possessions, hunger or greed in which a "brotherhood of man" would take precedence, as we could someday be "sharing all the world." I recall hearing this song at a spiritual center I attended a few days after 9/11. In that moment, as many tears were flowing, I could see that "Imagine" connects us to the intense yearning that we all share in our collective heart.

Of the people I interviewed for this book, Susan Bradbury from Bellingham, Washington, stands out as being passionate about cultivating peace on a global scale. I met her en route to Bali for the first Quest for Global Healing conference, in December 2004, and was drawn to her dynamic personality and contagious smile. With a sparkle in her eyes, she spoke about the Sound Essence Project she had developed to partner with others across the globe and promote peace through education, herbal medicine, sound, color and cultural communion. With that focus and her desire to help others out of material poverty, she subsequently developed a micro-lending project with a few women in Erdenet, Mongolia. This project benefited several families in this Mongolian community. Then, one night, she had a dream in which she wondered what children would imagine peace to look like. Soon after this she launched the project "What Does Peace Look Like?" and obtained cooperation from teachers in several countries. From their collective efforts a fascinating exhibition came together, including two hundred drawings from eight-to-ten-year-old schoolchildren around the world.

In 2006, Susan was presented with the Ambassador for Peace Award from the Universal Peace Federation and the International Federation for World Peace. Since receiving this award, she has been speaking about peace-making in many countries. As Susan followed her desire to make a difference, particularly in midlife, her life expanded, affording her opportunities to travel, meet great people, help and inspire others. She recently told me she is now involved in micro-lending projects in Burundi, Africa, as well as in Palestine and Israel. When Susan and I reflected in conversation about the year 2005, we realized that the exhibition about peace she created then co-incided with the twenty-fifth anniversary of the year John Lennon died. His message still reverberates in our hearts and through the actions of people like Susan.

Albert Einstein: Illuminations of the mind

> *Every day I remind myself that my inner and outer life are*
> *based on the labors of other men, living and dead,*
> *and that I must exert myself in order to give in the same*
> *measure as I have received and am still receiving.*
> —ALBERT EINSTEIN

In these words, Einstein acknowledges the importance of actively partici-pating in the circle of life that feeds the continuity in our society. This quote also points to the responsibility that we inherit from those who have forged new ideas and created innovations that have improved our quality of life. It is all too easy for us to forget the effort others have devoted to bringing about all of the things that now facilitate our lives.

Although Albert Einstein was not the man he wished he had been in his personal life, he felt, in the end, that he had made a sufficient contribution through his work. He was known as being inordinately devoted to his scientific quest, which was fulfilled as he developed and proved several groundbreaking theories. Evidently, his unrelenting commitment to his work yielded results equal to his efforts. What inspired me to include him here, in this constellation of extraordinary beings, is captured in one of his well-known quotations:

> A human being is a part of a whole, called by us "universe," a part limited in time and space. He experiences himself, his thoughts and feelings as something separated from the rest . . . a kind of optical delusion of his consciousness. This delusion is a kind of prison for us, restricting us to our personal desires and to affection for a few persons nearest to us. Our task must be to free ourselves from this prison by widening our circle of compassion to embrace all living creatures and the whole of nature in its beauty.

In this assertion, Einstein declared the universe to be an organic whole rather than a mechanistic entity. He urges us to see with the eyes of our spirit that we are interconnected in the oneness that links all beings. Einstein is also revered in my mind because he invited us to the realms of the imagination and the mysterious. He wrote: "The most beautiful thing we can experience is the mysterious. It is the source of all true art and all science. He to whom this emotion is a stranger, who can no longer pause to wonder and stand rapt in awe, is as good as dead: his eyes are closed." In our increasingly rushed and pragmatic world, we urgently need to reconnect with the mysterious, which helps us to preserve our humility before the vastness of the universe.

This humility then supports our evolution beyond the illusion that we can control the natural world. The mysterious commands respect and admiration for beauty, and it infuses more life force into our daily living. Without the ability to wonder, we can succumb to a routine-driven and drab existence in which our soul withers. As our alienation from our deeper self sets in, we are more likely to unconsciously numb our pain through materialism and other pursuits that fail to fulfill us.

Our inheritance from Mother Teresa

In this life, we cannot do great things.
We can only do small things with a great love.
—MOTHER TERESA

With an extraordinary commitment to her life's mission, Mother Teresa inspired us all through her deep humility, her faith and her far-reaching devotion. Looking at her growth through the hierarchy of needs developed by Maslow, it is evident that she led her whole life in the service of her spiritual needs, including the need to love selflessly.

Over the years, as she lived in accordance with the vow of poverty she had taken, she had many opportunities to bear witness to what real poverty was. She once stated that "loneliness and the feeling of being unwanted is the most terrible poverty." This real poverty was obvious in some of the homeless people she served, but Mother Teresa also saw this sort of poverty in the lives of some who had great material wealth. Through the course of her long life in the service of her charitable organization, she had the unique opportunity to be in the presence of both the poorest and the richest people in the world.

When she spoke in public, Mother Teresa affirmed that those who had been blessed with abundance had a responsibility to give to others who were much in need. She encouraged people to get involved with charitable causes and, according to the graces they received, to attend to the poor and lonely people near or far. In the beauty of her humility she revealed insights that carried such powerful wisdom. An example of this is when she stated: "It is not the magnitude of our actions but the amount of love that is put into them that matters."

Universal truths to take forward

Over the second half of the twentieth century, many other extraordinary people besides those mentioned have touched our lives and contributed greatly to our human evolution. In Canada, for example, Pierre Elliott Trudeau created a charter of rights that changed the Canadian landscape of human liberties forever. Decades earlier, women in Canada gained the important right to vote because of the ceaseless devotion of Nellie McClung, another leader who stood for justice and equality between genders. The foregoing overview of outstanding leaders reveals that their messages can be distilled into three universal truths most relevant for our unsettling times.

The first is that we share a primordial interconnectedness that many of us are scarcely aware of in daily living. Through their tireless work, these visionaries nourished the seeds of our awakening to our interdependence with all of life. This awakening can foster a new depth of compassion and generosity within us. In turn, this can counteract our tendency to shelter or isolate ourselves when we are exposed to our fear-inducing social and political climate. Interconnectedness is what compels people such as Susan Bradbury to reach out beyond borders in the cause of world peace.

The second truth that can transform us is the power of unconditional love; agape is a force that can overcome obstacles and barriers as nothing else can. Embodying this love, Mother Teresa proved its far-reaching power while she soothed the bodies and souls of thousands of people during her lifetime. When she said that the sick and poor people she served were really Jesus Christ in disguise, she meant that behind our appearances, roles or social status, we all inhabit a divine essence. This loving essence is the source of agape.

In our family, community or even in our workplace, many of us suffer as we hold onto grudges and unfinished business of all kinds. Accumulated resentments tend to drain our energies and lead us into apathy. As we take steps to release unfinished business, we can move beyond ego defenses and experience more joy along with the power of agape and collaboration. And in the face of our common challenge to experience unconditional self-acceptance and self-worth, unconditional love for ourselves can be enormously freeing and empowering.

The third timeless truth that emerges from these true leaders of our past is that commitment lies at the core of all extraordinary achievement or contribution. Part of the explanation for this can be found in the realm of quantum physics. When we understand the world as interrelated energy fields, we find that clarity of intentions, consistency and congruency together infuse energy and power in the fields in which we participate and are influenced. A widely cherished quotation by Goethe conveys what really occurs through commitment. He said, "The moment one definitely commits oneself, then Providence moves too. All sorts of things occur to help one that would never otherwise have occurred . . . unforeseen incidents, meetings, and material assistance, which no man could have dreamed would have come his way."

Thus, since the exceptional people described here were decisively committed, their convictions and influence still reverberate in the fields that connect their spirit to ours. In the universal yearnings that correspond with the highest desires of humanity, we can all find more resolve to help bring about peace, justice, love and a good quality of life for everyone. And as documented by Paul Hawken in *Blessed Unrest* (referred to in chapter 1), growing numbers across generations are getting involved through a proliferation of grassroots movements and organizations caring for the Earth and its people.

In the next section, I dispel some of the myths of midlife, explain what it means to hear the call of generativity, and invite you into an authentic homecoming journey. You will find several questions to ponder at the end of each chapter because, as Eugene Ionesco said, "It is not the answer that enlightens, but the question."

Question to ponder

- If one of your own wisest ancestors (or even a visionary leader such as Rosa Parks, Martin Luther King Jr., John Lennon, Albert Einstein or Mother Teresa) had words of wisdom to guide you in the next stage of your life, what would that person say?

The Inner Landscape
of Midlife

CHAPTER 3

Countering the Myths
of the Middle Passage

*The greatest discovery of my generation
is that human beings can alter their lives by
altering their attitudes of mind.*

—William James

As a prominent psychologist of the nineteenth century, William James knew that the discovery of the power of the mind was indeed a significant breakthrough. This idea—that we can change our lives by changing our thinking—prevails in the realms of personal and professional development today. To this end, this chapter aims at shifting attitudes and dispelling false collective beliefs so that we can free ourselves to live "full on" in midlife or as an elder. By living "full on," I mean tapping the greatness of our potential, moving beyond limiting beliefs and growing wisely into new realms of self-awareness, creativity and contribution. To live this way we must courageously address any dissonance in our lives, such as a lack of congruency between what we value/love and where/how we use our time and energies in daily life.

At some point in midlife most of us feel torn by competing commitments. At once, we want to remain responsible to our obligations yet free ourselves into new endeavors. We want to turn our dreams into a new reality yet retain our habitual ways of living. Clearly, at this time we cannot help but question ourselves, our values, our work, wondering if this is what our life is really meant to be. Even when we are eager to move past our own previously perceived limitations, outdated beliefs seeping in from our social surroundings can impede our movement forward. Often inadvertently, the people in our lives act out of protectiveness while they unconsciously pressure us into remaining the same so that they can maintain the status quo.

As I see it, aging is inevitable but getting old is optional. Evidently, if we become overly concerned about our slowly diminishing abilities as we get older, we will set our minds to age prematurely. Our generation is increasingly motivated to stay vibrantly active, to keep evolving and channeling their "fire in the belly" toward concrete actions. In great numbers, we are taking steps to become or remain in a dynamic alignment with our body, mind and spirit as the years go by. Join me in discarding remnants of obsolete ideas about midlife so we can better create positive shifts and participate, each in our own way, in the betterment of our society.

Tapping the power of the holistic middle-aged brain

In the vast diversity that characterizes boomers, significant differences exist in the perception of middle age. Across the generations, some people perceive the middle years as that short plateau after which "everything goes downhill." You have likely heard someone in middle age unknowingly reinforce this myth by excusing himself for having "a senior moment" while being unable to remember something. The idea behind this myth is that our brain, our cognitive abilities and our memory all deteriorate more or less rapidly from our late forties onwards.

Numerous studies in recent years have examined the brain during middle age and elder years; the old adage of "use it or lose it" is turning out to be true. And from the fields of quantum physics and new biology, it is now widely accepted that our thoughts and expectations have significant power to affect our well-being. We also know that creating less stress and more holistic well-being for ourselves requires more than just positive thinking.

In his book *The Biology of Belief*, Bruce Lipton explains the interdependence between our conscious and subconscious mind in relation to our capacity to optimize our health. He also quotes numerous studies that support his observations about mind over matter in the realm of health. In chapter 8, on well-being, you will find additional examples of the power of body-mind interconnectivity.

While some of us, particularly women in menopause, experience occasional memory challenges such as trying to remember names, we should not get overly concerned about these common changes. Evidently, if you expect declining mental abilities with age and gradually diminish your level of involvement in life and in mind-stimulating activities, you are more likely to instigate such a decline. In other words, we tend to get what we expect. Let us then avoid drifting into a self-fulfilling prophecy.

When we take responsibility for keeping our brain thriving, we can reap the benefits of our efforts far into the later years. I recently read in a local newspaper about a 92-year-old man who was tired of his embarrassing illiteracy and successfully taught himself to read. My dear friend Jan Furst, a resident of Bowen Island in B.C., taught himself to use a computer in his late eighties. So the old myth of not being able to "teach an old dog new tricks" should also be discarded as an obsolete belief. Although it is true that some of our less used neural pathways tend to atrophy as the years go by, there is much we can do to retain our sharpness of mind.

Also encouraging, recent discoveries in neuroscience show that the brain is more flexible and adaptable than was previously thought. Some studies suggest, as reported by Dr. Gene Cohen in *Newsweek*, that "the brain's left and right hemispheres become better integrated during the middle years, making way for greater creativity." It turns out that our generation's creative surge referred to in chapter 1 is a manifestation of positive biological changes.

Time magazine reported in early 2006 that Dr. George Bartozokis, a neurologist from UCLA, had conducted a study involving 300 healthy subjects from ages 18 to 75 and hundreds of older people who suffered from Alzheimer's and Parkinson's diseases. With the use of magnetic resonance, Bartozokis studied the volume and distribution of the subjects' white matter, which is mostly made of conductive nerve strands and fatty sheaths of myelin. Throughout our lives, he says, fresh layers of myelin sheathing are laid down in the brain. According to Bartozokis, "The brain spends decades upgrading itself from a dial-up Internet to a high-speed version." This process, which includes the continuous production of new myelin sheathing, is not fully completed until we are in our late forties or early fifties.

Bartozokis found that the healthy adults had the most myelin in the frontal and temporal lobes, the two areas of the brain that form the seat of sophisticated thought. The myth-busting evidence is that as we go through midlife, different regions of our brain start pulling together more efficiently "to make the whole organ work better than the sum of its parts." Benefits of this more interconnected brain include new surges of creativity as well as more holistic ways of understanding and seeing the world. And along with the desire to create comes the loosening of inhibitions. Perhaps you are experiencing this in your own life, noticing your self-expression coming to the fore in whole new ways.

Surges of creativity and wisdom seeking expression

With this newly optimized, more connected brain, many of us in midlife are seeking to liberate our creativity in various aspects of daily living. The increased number of connections between the left and the right hemispheres is providing us access to new, larger perspectives. This broader, more encompassing vantage point often gives rise to greater empathy and compassion for others. And with greater connectivity between the left and the right brain, the logical, linear and the intuitive, creative propensities are coming into harmony, often producing more emotional stability. This is what enables us to better inhabit qualities of equanimity: becoming more poised, less reactive and more connected to a deep inner knowing, a newfound wisdom.

In a *Newsweek* article, Gene Cohen, MD, gave the example of an editor at the top of his career with a New York publishing company who, in late middle age, felt like a "changed man." He had formerly been critical and brusque, often alienating those around him. But in midlife his emotional development had finally caught up with his intellectual development, resulting in more empathy and a newfound mastery of interpersonal communications. He changed from being a brilliant but brittle loner into a wise person channeling his capacities to help through mentoring and by mediating conflicts when the need arose.

As for emerging creativity, stories regularly show up these days about boomers turning these surges into bold visions, actions and innovative enterprises. This time of life provides an opportunity to rediscover talents that were left behind at the apex of youth. An example of this has occurred in my own family. My sister in Montreal recently rekindled her old passion for theatre and is enjoying the thrill of acting on stage again in her fifties. And within a year of recovering my own artistic talents, colorful paintings I have created are now adorning walls in a few homes across our continent.

The second adolescence misjudgment

Another expression of common misunderstandings about midlife is that of judging a man or woman in their fifties as acting like the stereotypical teenager. Such a person might seem to care less about their family responsibilities, become overly interested in their appearance, spend too much, or frivolously launch themselves into new endeavors on a whim. At such a time, many of us appear to be contrarian to others as we "rock the boat" at work or at home. This is often a reflection of the friction within as we question our assumptions, expectations and beliefs, most of which have not yielded the happiness we expected.

This misjudgment is particularly harmful when it is used by family members or co-workers to mock or humiliate a person facing the ground-shaking issues and concerns of midlife. Being subjected to such mockery is particularly painful if we have a sincere desire to heal the incongruence that may have become intolerable in our life. When our authentic self is dying to edge out and lead the way, we do not want to hear negative comments that make us doubt our capacity to harness our courage and make positive changes. Of course, by this time of life, we usually have many responsibilities at home and at work, and we should refrain from suddenly "busting loose," thereby causing hardship or anxiety for those around us. Deep down, when the midlife passage generates confusion and growing pains, we are best to communicate openly with others near us, lest we become more alienated, conflicted or depressed.

One of my current coaching clients found himself in just such a difficult place while trying to listen to and reconnect with his core self in midlife. He was no longer satisfied with his successful career and wanted a change. His restless anxiety was exacerbated by his wife's comments that he should "grow up" and get over his "second adolescence." He was also warned against going on a "wild goose chase" while exploring to discover a new, more authentic vocation. As he felt the promptings of his deeper self, he was confused by the messages from those around him wanting him to continue being the same person and playing the same roles he had played for years. He yearned to reinvent himself, open to his creativity and step beyond people's expectations of him.

After we worked together for some time, this client made a foundational choice, thereby altering the course of his work life. A stream of actions naturally followed, appeasing his restless anxiety while further engaging him toward a new, satisfying purpose. His wife now better understands, and she is supportive of her husband's new direction.

Reinterpreting the "midlife crisis"

One dictionary definition of crisis is "a crucial stage or turning point in the course of something." The middle passage *is* a turning point, a developmental transition rich with new potential. Western mainstream culture still upholds the belief that when we reach our forties or fifties, we are supposed to have settled into a profession, a continuing routine, and a predictable way of life. Placed in historical context, this belief may have been functional when our life expectancy was much shorter. Understandably, we do crave more stability over time, but we also need to keep moving forward on our developmental path as we respond to changes arising within and around us. If we want real vitality in midlife, we must create a dynamic balance between sameness and stability versus renewal and creativity. Clinging to "same old" patterns is a fear-based habit that stems from our resistance to the process of transition, which is a typical initial reaction to change.

In his book *The Way of Transition*, William Bridges writes that, paradoxically, even just to achieve continuity in the present, we must be willing to shift and continuously readjust in response to changes from within and without. Bridges further explains that transition is the necessary process through which we come to terms with change. Discerning between a developmental transition such as midlife and a reactive transition such as recovering from the loss of a spouse, Bridges states that such processes includes three phases. The initial stage of letting go of the old or current situation typically brings on a fearful state. Managing the in-between, neutral zone of the transition means that we must sort through confusion, doubt and conflicting emotions. In the third stage, we again experience some apprehension as we encounter the uncertainties of making a new beginning. Clearly, we must patiently listen inward and seek appropriate support as we go through these three stages during a developmental transition or a major change occasioned by divorce or retirement. If we become immobilized by fears, we may succumb to inertia and apathy, which is sure to lead to regrets later.

To the extent that you harness the inner life force that surges from your authentic self in midlife, you can overcome fears as you walk the creative tension between the old and the new. Think about a toddler attempting to walk for the first time. A child will experience many painful falls in the process, yet we do not call this stage a "crisis of mobility." That is because we know this period of growth includes a series of failed attempts that will lead to success in the end. Sometimes in our middle passage, we experience setbacks similar to those a toddler experiences while learning to walk. Trying to live in greater congruence and integrity with our true self can be hindered by clutter of our past conditioning, the hectic busyness of our lives and the weight of unresolved emotional baggage. The rest of this chapter as well as chapter 5 identify some of the travails of finding our footing again through this time of life.

Facing the true challenge presented by midlife

The middle years find some of us still eager to achieve more status and financial success, often driven by our basic needs, our family responsibilities or ego-centered values. But gradually, we may become more ill at ease below the veneer of our worldly success. Sometimes, as our inner voice awakens and tries to get our attention, we resist and react by distracting ourselves in various ways. You may have observed examples of this around you: self-destructive thoughts, infidelity, growing compulsivity or even alcohol abuse to drown out a sense of meaninglessness or feeling lost.

In his book *The Middle Passage: From Misery to Meaning in Midlife*, James Hollis highlights the fundamental truths that are characteristic of midlife. One sobering truth is that we tend to repeat, with growing anxiety and decreasing efficacy, the patterns of behavior we have developed to keep our midlife awakening urgency at bay. We may find, for example, that some of the new things we buy compulsively satisfy us for shorter and shorter spans of time. I recall observing this in one of my coaching clients, who bought a fancy sports car he wanted. The thrill of the newness wore off quickly, following which he recognized his habit of trying to fill an inner void with new material acquisitions.

Another resounding truth Hollis discusses is that through the middle passage our soul wants to be heard, to be honored, and it asks us to awaken to its truth and wisdom. We are at first unsettled by this new life energy surging from the soul. With this force comes an undeniable and disruptive urgency that, writes Hollis, tends to cause "anxiety when acknowledged and depression when suppressed." This "enormous force" often shows up as a kind of "fire in the belly," a surge of energy accompanied by a desire to get to know and express ourselves in a profound new way. This is the force of greatness composer Giacomo Puccini referred to when he said, "The conscious purposeful appropriation of one's own soul-forces is the supreme secret. . . . Then I feel the burning desire and intense resolve to create something worthwhile."

The following passage from Elaine Pagels' *Gnostic Gospels* captures the essence of the transformational opportunity of midlife: "If you bring forth what is within you, what you bring forth will save you. If you do not bring forth what is within you, what you do not bring forth will destroy you." Behind the self we have presented to others, our core self now urges us to remove the dissonance in our life and become more alive by embracing our authentic self first and foremost. We suddenly realize that if we continue to edit out what we think does not match the expectations of others, we risk our life resembling a bland novel, devoid of freshness, spark and imagination.

My friend Brigitte, now in her late fifties, recently said to me that she has experienced a rebirth as a result of becoming more deeply honest with herself and others. Paradoxically, when we follow our inner impulses and commit to being true to ourselves, we naturally open the path to our "soul-forces" as we also create deepening paths of relating with others.

When a new vocation calls

For those who have been devoted to fulfilling work or engaging causes, midlife may still be a turning point at which we recommit with more boldness and passion to our occupation. For others, yearning for change in midlife arises from a desire to shift their work so it becomes more like a vocation than a career or a job. Through this change we intuitively sense the possibility of better using our talents and challenge ourselves anew to "bring forth" what is within us. If this urge arises with clarity as a result of a re-evaluation and a sense of irresistible calling, we are wise to move through the transition phases and act on these inner promptings. In chapter 5 you will read about Larry Robinson, a man who did heed his inner voice in midlife and became courageously engaged in new rewarding endeavors. What follows here is an example of a friend's failure to heed the voice within that urged him to let go of the old and enter into something new.

This friend, whom I'll call John, took a job as a groundskeeper at a university in his late twenties during an employment gap at the start of a career as a counselor. In his early forties, having stayed in this manual labor job for more than fifteen years, he felt an enormous restlessness, wanted to further his studies and return to his earlier interest in working with people as a helping professional. John knew that he liked supporting people, and he remembered that as a counselor he was getting good at helping others to understand themselves. He talked about embarking on this new career with his wife and others, many of whom discouraged him from making the change. Although he and his wife had no children and no major financial obligations, John hesitated to move on for fear of facing financial uncertainty for some time. After a couple of years of doubt and indecision, John decided not to make the change he really wanted deep down. He would remain in his manual labor job until retirement. He rationalized his passive choice by saying that his midlife ambitions were "not realistic" and that he was probably too old to change the course of his work life. Having stayed on this path of least effort, John resigned himself and remained in his slowly narrowing comfort zone. When I saw him a couple of years later, I sensed that apathy and sorrowful regrets had made themselves at home within him.

Now, at age 60, John is planning to retire next year but is anxious, knowing that his options are more limited now than when he was more energetic in his forties. It is indeed more challenging to rediscover a sense of purpose after thirty years in an unfulfilling job that led to self-alienation. Certainly that work paid the bills, but staying in it for so long caused John to forfeit the purposeful use of his real talents.

To avoid getting stuck in the neutral stage of a transition or to end up dwelling in resignation, we need to allow ourselves to hear, reflect upon and act on what really calls us in midlife. Rather than settling for the easiest and most comfortable route, we must continually and intently shape the course of our own happiness. Just as a toddler cannot be stopped from learning to walk, we cannot stop wanting to use our full potential and to grow by challenging ourselves appropriately. This is what leads to real happiness and enjoyment of life. The middle passage can be treacherous terrain, but let us be attentive to its exciting potentiality, the new energies we can harness, and the optimized brain that we have developed. Between the dreams and ambitions we once held dear and the deeper aspirations and integrity we could now embrace lies the foundation of our new, more authentic way of being.

Developmental opportunities

With a deeper understanding of the middle passage, we come to see that this time of life actually offers us new developmental opportunities. These opportunities, further explained in chapter 14, include the following:

- Reconnect with and listen to our authentic self.
- Slow down enough to enjoy life because we are more aware of its preciousness and its precariousness.
- Express ourselves: free our voices and our creativity.
- Reassess our purpose and re-align our values with integrity.
- Connect more deeply with those we love and develop new relationships that enable us to see ourselves in a new light.
- Simplify our life so that less energy goes into acquiring and maintaining material things as their importance diminishes.
- Harness the spirit of generativity as a wind in our sails while we set out to make a difference in the lives of others.

The summary of practical applications in chapter 14 suggests practices to help you embrace the above opportunities.

Guiding principles and ideas for the homecoming journey are offered in chapter 5. But first, the next chapter is designed to help you understand and respond to the call of generativity. This is an essential element of this developmental stage: the energy awakening within giving rise to the desire to make a difference in the lives of others. As you read examples of people who have responded to this call, you will learn how this energy or life force can lead to new depth of meaning and fulfillment in your own life.

Questions to ponder

- What beliefs do you hold about midlife?
- How do these beliefs impact you, serve your best interests or undermine you?
- What do you see as your most significant challenge in your present or upcoming transition into midlife and/or re-engagement, still commonly known as retirement?
- As you contemplate the following quotation, where do you see yourself in the balance of acting/planning and dreaming/believing in your life?

> *To accomplish great things, we must not only act,*
> *but also dream; not only plan, but also believe.*
> — ANATOLE FRANCE

- What do you believe or dream that you have yet to accomplish with your life?

CHAPTER 4

The Call of Generativity

We make a living by what we get,
but we make a life by what we give.

—Sir Winston Churchill

With an intense fervor, the spirit of generativity is awakening in many of us as we walk the midlife passage. The stories in this chapter are about people who have harnessed this expansive desire to give and serve as they grow through their personal journey. Here you will read about what fosters or hinders our response to generativity in the context of our social and psycho-spiritual development. The chapter also touches on research studies that support the multiple benefits of giving, which include longevity and enhanced wellness.

Not surprisingly, those who shared their stories of generativity with me exhibited a buoyant kind of vitality. In a colorful restaurant on one cold rainy evening, the Vancouver educator Janey Talbot warmed my heart with her story. Janey and her friends Violet and Doreen joined a Learning Journey in Africa in 2007 with the U.S.-based Berkana Institute. After describing the highlights of her travels in South Africa, Janey spoke affectionately about some of the African women she met during her visits to preschools in both inner-city Johannesburg and Zimbabwe. Among them was Patricia, a Kufundee in Zimbabwe, who was particularly radiant as a devoted preschool teacher eager to learn more about supporting young children's development. A spark of friendship between Patricia and Janey quickly grew into a bond, which then ignited in Janey a desire to contribute to Patricia's growth and education.

During our restaurant conversation, Janey was animated as she talked about her friendships and the special moments of her journey. A surge of inspired passion crossed her face when she exclaimed: "Once I realized that we're all one, I could not do nothing. And I was concerned that if I did not act on this impulse now, I might not initiate anything once I returned home to my busy life." While still in Africa, Janey and her friends started the process of helping Patricia and Mathebedi, a South African preschool teacher, to apply for visas to come to Canada for an educational visit. Upon returning home, Janey, Violet and Doreen raised funds for the trip by giving slide shows and selling photo cards. In their own countries, meanwhile, Patricia and Mathebedi used their courage and persistence to take all of the necessary actions to obtain their visas. A few months later, they landed in Vancouver, where they were warmly greeted by their Canadian friends, who hosted the two preschool teachers for two weeks. During their stay, they were exposed to Canada's natural wonders, to Canadian culture and to the best preschools in the area by Janey, Doreen and Violet, who delighted in the company of such special guests.

Having added calendars to the fundraising products, Janey was pleased to report that regular donations, personal contributions and sales were enabling her to send funds for the purchase of equipment and supplies to the African preschools where Patricia and Mathebedi work. Regular e-mails help to maintain strong bonds between these women who share a special affection that bridges the distance between continents.

As Janey and I concluded our conversation that night, we talked about the profound kind of fulfillment that comes from helping others across our beloved planet. Together, we delighted in the realization that when we have an experiential knowing of the oneness we all share, we cannot help but heed the call of generativity. In chapter 14, you can read my own joyful story of generosity: the sponsoring and hosting of a Balinese person to visit Canada for an educational opportunity in the summer of 2007.

Living forward into generativity

In the middle of the past century, the psychoanalyst and leader in the field of human development Erik Erikson developed an approach to psychosocial development comprising eight life stages. Through his work, his research and his observations, Erikson recognized that in middle age we experience the call of generativity: a natural propensity to widen our circle of care beyond ourselves and our family and to make a difference in other people's lives. As Erikson and his wife, Joan Erikson, elaborated their developmental model in the 1980s, they added a ninth stage, to address the period of old age from our eighties onwards.

In chapter 2, I mentioned that Albert Einstein urged us to expand our circle of care and to free ourselves from the delusion of our perceived separateness from others. To repeat, he said, "This delusion is a kind of prison for us, restricting us to our personal desires and to affection for a few persons nearest to us. Our task must be to free ourselves from this prison by widening our circle of compassion to embrace all living creatures and the whole of nature in its beauty."

In addition to recognizing this impulse to expand our caring for others, a sentiment echoed by Einstein, Erik Erikson found that midlife is characterized by the opposing inner forces of generativity and stagnation. If you have felt generativity beckoning, you may also be aware of a latent fear of inactivity and meaninglessness. The author Anaïs Nin said that "life's opportunities shrink or expand in proportion to one's courage." This is akin to what Erikson warned about: if we overlook our developmental tasks and succumb to inertia, we are likely to find ourselves in a sorrowful place of stagnation and resignation.

In midlife particularly, if our areas of involvement contract rather than expand, or we are more guarded rather than wholeheartedly engaged with others, we tend to become more self-absorbed as a result. Proportionally, our relatively minor concerns about ourselves or others in our immediate surroundings may become magnified, because there is not much else on which to place our attention. But if we make giving back and infusing our actions with love a greater priority, we will experience fresh opportunities along with renewed energy. In this way we can joyfully harness the creative tension between the opposing poles of generativity and stagnation that typically arise in the middle passage.

People often experience the spirit of generosity with an almost visceral momentous energy, as Janey Talbot did, but it does require courage to initiate a course of action and commit to following through. Yet, paradoxically, drawing from our well of courage stimulates its effervescence, and we are further emboldened to stay the course even as we encounter challenges. Soon we find that our efforts are well compensated by the new depth of meaning that enriches our life.

For those who wonder how or where to start giving back or helping, a multitude of options awaits discovery when we answer the call of generativity arising within. Whether expressed through a shift in your attitude or your work orientation, through volunteering, or through finding another way to help, to mentor, to sponsor or otherwise support, the possibilities are endless. Allow me to revisit the toddler analogy I presented in chapter 3. The child learning to walk does not ask herself whether there is any place worth going before practicing the skill of walking. That child starts to walk propelled by curiosity and the natural course of her development. As toddlers take their new steps, they are further enthralled by the many enjoyable things and people to get closer to. Likewise, generativity is a process born out of an inner growth and evolution, in midlife and eldership especially.

With your curiosity as a faithful friend, and your deepening inner guidance, open your heart to what really touches you and let it lead the way. Just as your legs and feet led the way many decades ago, your heart and your mind will lead you to your own best course of action in alignment with your particular gifts and abilities. While you keep exploring the inner chambers of your heart and hone your talents and knowledge, the clouds of doubt on your path will dissipate as clarity of purpose arises.

Removing hindrances to generativity

Although many of us awaken to the desire to give back, we can be hindered by various factors, among them financial insecurity, the pursuit of material wealth, and anxiety fed by the media and world events. Fear of material scarcity lurks in the minds of some boomers, preventing them from living fully and generously. Such a fear will cause many of us to conserve our resources, perhaps more than necessary, or retreat within ourselves, closing ourselves off from the needs that we may otherwise respond to. Persistent fear of lack also causes some people to continue accumulating greater material abundance while never really reaching a state of satisfaction.

According to *The Soul of Money*, by Lynne Twist, who spent more than two decades fundraising for the Hunger Project, the vast majority of funds received by charitable organizations are from middle-class families. Sadly, it seems that the more we have, the more we want to keep and the less we are inclined to give of our resources or of ourselves. Of course, there are numerous exceptions. The philanthropist Warren Buffett is one among many, regularly giving away millions to selected foundations. But among the wealthy, those who are trapped in pursuit of more or worry about lack often miss the opportunity to experience contentment.

Other hindrances to generosity arise from the current sociopolitical climate, which generates, and is infused by, fear and anxiety. Our culture is fraught with angst-producing messages coming from media and from some politicians. These messages have an isolating effect on some of us; we want to stay close to home with the ones we most love and want to protect. It is natural to retreat to a place of safety when we perceive danger. And when we are preoccupied with safety needs, we are less likely to move forward toward higher needs on the path of development. According to Abraham Maslow's hierarchy of needs, we first strive to meet our basic physiological, safety and social needs. Then we naturally gravitate toward fulfilling our cognitive, aesthetic, self-realization and spiritual needs. This model supports Erikson's developmental view that includes transcending our ego-centered, more mundane preoccupations to serve our spiritual needs as we expand into generative endeavors in midlife.

But most of us do not necessarily progress smoothly toward these highest needs. At times, we may be set back by financial challenges that bring our attention down to survival and safety needs. Furthermore, in our current stressful times and overwhelmingly fast-paced lives, many of us are operating in survival mode, just striving to maintain our sanity along with our health. For some, a health crisis may exacerbate already stressful circumstances. But adversity or health challenges can also propel us forward and help us shift our priorities according to new perspectives, as you'll read in chapter 8 on wellness. Depending on our faith, the support we enlist and the inner resourcefulness we harness, overcoming difficult times is often conducive to reshaping one's life according to the timeless wisdom of the heart.

Clearly, as we advance on our life path, various challenges and humbling failures can serve to sharpen our ability to empathize with others and experience compassion. Recognition in midlife of life's precariousness also motivates us to respond to prompting of the self-realization and of the spiritual needs within. These two levels of needs converge to generate the desire to give back. Mahatma Gandhi affirmed this when he said, "To find yourself, lose yourself in the service of others." A signpost that we are entering the realms of our higher needs is the realization that, as Janey said, "we're all one."

Studies support the benefits of giving

In their book *The Power of Giving*, co-authors Azim Jamal and Harvey McKinnon point out that as we reach out to meet the needs of others, we attend to our own self-realization and spiritual needs. I concur with their conclusion that giving also leads to having more joy, more lightness of being, stronger relationships and more internal peace. Recent research studies reveal that helping others also enhances our holistic health.

In *Why Good Things Happen to Good People*, the authors Stephen Post and Jill Neimark write about the different ways we can support and love others. From generative actions such as volunteering to providing empathic listening, compassion and support, Post and Neimark remind us of the importance of giving and its benefits for the giver. They refer to several studies that link generosity to well-being and longevity. One was completed by Doug Oman of the University of California at Berkeley. Oman followed nearly two thousand individuals over the age of fifty-five for five years. Results revealed that those who volunteered for two or more organizations had an impressive 44 percent lower likelihood of dying within the time span of the study. This result held even after accounting for other factors such as physical health, amount of exercise, gender and marital status. This reduced mortality rate surpasses the benefits of exercising four times per week, which rates at 30 percent mortality reduction.

Aside from the well-documented benefits of volunteering in the community, it turns out that helping friends, relatives and others by providing emotional support also contributes significantly to longevity. Such was the conclusion of another study included in Post and Neimark's book, about the work of Stephanie Brown, a psychologist at the University of Michigan who studied 423 older couples for five years. After adjusting for age, health, gender and other factors, Brown found that those who provided no significant support to others were more than twice as likely to die in that five-year period. Being supportive of those around us is relatively easy, especially if we make this an intentional part of our life. Yet the benefits of extending this kind of caring can be easily underestimated. Read more about ways of caring for each other in chapter 7, on relationships beyond the workplace.

As you walk the inner landscape of midlife and beyond with the intention to be engaged in a generous way of life, you are likely to develop more appreciation for all that you have been given. Such is the experience of gratitude. The author Melody Beattie captures the power of gratitude with the following words, which I found in author Azim Khamisa's *Peace and Freedom Newsletter*.

> Gratitude unlocks the fullness of life. It turns what we have into enough, and more. It turns denial into acceptance, chaos to order, confusion to clarity. It can turn a meal into a feast, a house into a home, a stranger into a friend. Gratitude makes sense of our past, brings peace for today, and creates a vision for tomorrow.

In his book *Beauty: The Invisible Embrace*, John O'Donohue states that gratitude is the appropriate response to being abundantly blessed, as most of us have been in our generation. The revered scholar and author Brother David Steindl-Rast also speaks and writes eloquently about gratitude and thankfulness. He says that contrary to what most of us tend to believe, we do not feel grateful because we are happy; rather, we become happy through practicing the art of gratitude. In this practice we are inwardly filled with appreciation, the overflowing of which compels us to turn to one another. Embodying graciousness invites the experience of blessings into one's life, which in turn compels us into deeper realms of generosity.

Reflecting on our motives to help

"If you are coming to help me, you are wasting your time. But if you are coming because your liberation is bound up with mine, then let us work together." This indigenous saying quoted by Lynne Twist in *The Soul of Money* cautions us against any inclination to help *save* "poor" people because we feel sorry for them. If we are motivated by pity, a sense of superiority or a patriarchal attitude, we diminish those we aim to serve. At times, the circumstances surrounding people we want to help may have stripped from them their dignity. As we give of ourselves or our resources, we must see the recipients of our help as being whole, worthy and eventually capable of making proactive choices to improve their own lives. In this way through our giving we support self-reliance and a healthy kind of interdependence. When we give from a place of full engagement, courageously confronting the societal and institutional challenges we face as a species, then we greatly contribute to humanity.

For some, wanting to give back arises out of a heartfelt desire to help bring about a better future for the generations to come. This sense of generational responsibility is emerging as a strong motivator among some boomers and elders. For example, the organization For the GrandChildren of the Earth was founded in 2006 in Seattle, Washington, by Victor Bremson and Rich Henry, who shared the same passion for embracing generational responsibility in action. Through their newsletter, workshops and symposiums, Bremson, Henry and their team are stimulating awareness about the urgency of our global crises. As they provide information and inspiration, they build community among boomers and elders eager to take actions in response to the eleventh hour we are facing. Recognizing that there is great power, joy and synergy in joining with others, their organization helps individuals to partake in some of the initiatives aimed at bettering our world for the grandchildren of the Earth.

Heeding the call of generativity across the distance

In responding to the call to serve, we frequently feel a surge of energy and engagement that is revitalizing to our soul. Such was the experience of Carsten Henningsen, an Oregon resident and the chair of Portfolio 21, which specializes in environmental and community development investing. Carsten moved into generative action in a greater way than he had before following the large-scale disaster caused by the tsunami in Southeast Asia in December 2004.

While completing a degree in Asian studies in the early 1980s, Carsten went to a monastery and attended a university in Sri Lanka. In subsequent years he maintained a close bond with some of the people he had met in Sri Lanka, particularly those involved in community service. When he heard of the devastation in the wake of the tsunami, he felt a profound impulse to respond. "I remember sitting on the couch, shocked by the news, and then suddenly realizing that I had to go. So I jumped up and got on the phone to make travel arrangements." After contacting several people he knew in the United States, Carsten collected generous donations, then went to Sri Lanka to assist in the reconstruction of a school and attend to other needs that came to his attention.

Upon his return to the United States, Carsten founded Community Friends, an organization that has partnered with a nongovernmental organization in Sri Lanka. The group's current projects include addressing malnutrition of children, supporting small family enterprises with innovative financing solutions, and providing educational scholarships. In July 2007, Carsten shared with me that, to his amazement, the organization's meal program had been working very well and that over fifty thousand hot lunches had been served to children in the Ulla village in Sri Lanka. The school principal of that village told Carsten that this meal program was the most meaningful help they had received since the tsunami. "Thanks to a special grant," Carsten said, "we were able to build a kitchen as well. Before the kitchen, 150 meals a day were cooked on a campfire."

While in Sri Lanka, Carsten was also compelled by compassion to address the plight of young village women. Through Community Friends, he provides opportunities for young women to overcome poverty by creating sustainable livelihoods for themselves. He explained: "Through social enterprise, we are using micro-venture capital to create micro-entrepreneurs, providing financial empowerment by way of access to capital that would otherwise be unavailable. We are focusing on a segment of the population that would likely be overlooked by existing micro-lending programs. And most importantly, this segment of the village population is also the most vulnerable."

In Carsten, as in Susan Bradbury, whose story is told in chapter 2, generativity has spread its wings, enabling them to keep widening their circle of care in the spirit of service. In the summer of 2007, Carsten traveled to Cambodia. After his return he wrote to me by e-mail:

> Although I had no intention of this happening, I was led to a language school for the poorest of children run by a man who was raised by monks after 22 members of his family were killed by the Khmer Rouge. Some of the children have HIV and several have already died. The schoolteacher hopes that following his teachings of English and Japanese, the students will be able to find jobs in the growing tourist business. He started this school three years ago and has three students who are now employed in hotels, etc. Most of the children are 7–13 years old. The school has no walls, just a dirt floor and roof. They have no books, paper or pencils, just a whiteboard.

Carsten saw this teacher in action and said that he was engaging, attentive and effective. Wanting to help with the school's needs, Carsten asked how much it would cost to get books, paper and pencils for all of the sixty students. "One hundred and fifty dollars," said the teacher, and this amount would even cover some clothes for the poorest children. Led by Carsten, Community Friends is now branching out to Cambodia. The website for this organization is listed in the resource section.

Carsten's dedication and humanitarian work are inspiring. I was touched by a comment he made during one of our conversations about leading a meaningful life that brings true fulfillment. When I asked him to tell me in a few words what his life purpose is, he paused for a moment and said: "It's about relieving the suffering of others."

During my research for this book, I met several people who drew my attention to individuals, such as Carsten, who are making a significant difference in the world. Cedric Monteiro, a resident of Vancouver, Canada, creates outstanding documentaries for the Canadian Broadcasting Corporation. After completing a documentary about the nonprofit organization Walking Together for Health and Development, he told me about the tireless work of its founder, Susan Smith, in Mexico, and I made plans to speak with her.

In 1996, at the start of midlife, Susan returned to Mexico with her eight-year-old son, after completing a doctorate in community health and development and social participation. Exhausted from her extended studies and her work as an assistant professor at McMaster University in Ontario, Susan sought out a place to reflect and recuperate. She was drawn to the community of Tlamacazapa, a village of approximately 6,150 people located in the rocky mountains of central Mexico. There she gradually became aware of the multiple problems of daily living among the villagers, and she was particularly moved to help the local women free themselves from the grip of poverty and oppression. "It took a good three to four years to gain a good understanding of the issues," Susan told me.

In this village where residents are full of suspicion and culturally induced fears, the problems are complex and pervasive. They include malnutrition, deaths of small children, illnesses, and extreme fatigue in women particularly. In addition, violence and beatings often result from alcohol abuse by men. During her first few years in the community, Susan experienced many difficult moments and she felt like giving up. Yet her character strengths and the strong bonds she had created helped her stay, determined to persevere and create opportunities for villagers to have a better life.

In the face of tough challenges, Susan and a growing team of international volunteers gradually developed an organization and programs to respond to the needs of the community and especially to those of its women. Since its start in 1997, Caminamos Juntos Para Salud y Desarrollo (Walking Together for Health and Development) has taken a holistic approach to community development that focuses on three main areas. Self-sufficiency is fostered through income-generating programs, including women's weaving and quilting groups, midwifery training, masonry skills for men and small-business development. Other programs focus on rebuilding trusting relationships and a renewed sense of community by studying and working together to construct physical infrastructure, such as rainwater catchment tanks and toilets.

The third area of focus relates to both education and health. It aims to strengthen villagers by raising awareness about how to prevent infant mortality, birth defects and water contamination. This program also helps villagers form new friendships and learn new skills, such as reading. A free primary-care clinic and low-cost dental care are part of this program. What is more, by February 2008, Susan had enabled thirteen village women to visit Canada, where they could be exposed to new experiences, learn different perspectives and gain confidence in their own voices. As they return home empowered by their experience, these women are part of a growing critical mass helping to transform a village culture that has been toxic for several decades.

Although as a young adult Susan was inclined toward service, working almost continuously in different settings, it is in midlife that she felt the generative impulse to start this organization. As she recognized in herself the skills needed to be effective and called on her inner strengths as never before, she was able to persist with the work over the past ten years. There are still many complex problems in Tlamacazapa, but Susan knows that her life has purpose, and she is fulfilled by the many small shifts she sees around her. When I asked what keeps her engaged, Susan said, "Many times, I feel a sense of achievement when a woman stands up and gives her opinion, saying something she would not have been able to say before."

Aside from the focus on very practical solutions to improve the quality of life in Tlamacazapa, "the real work," Susan explained, is in addressing the roots of oppression caused by influential forces and ingrained beliefs. As our conversation came to a close, she pointed out that the internal oppression she sees in this Mexican village is something that exists in different forms across all cultures. "The loneliness, high incidence of depression, and the meaninglessness we see in the richer countries are also symptoms of internal oppression," she said. It is true that when we are bound up in mistrust or limiting beliefs, feeling unloved or that we have lost our way, we are disconnected from the inner light that can otherwise illuminate the path toward a truly meaningful life. Without that inner connection, we are unaware of our interdependence as human beings and of the responsibility to help that arises from having been born in an affluent society. Without the light of that awareness, we are blind to the greatness and the love inside waiting to be released and channeled into purposeful actions.

If you are feeling the spark of generativity stirring within but wonder where to start, be patient—yet don't waste a moment. It is easy to be overwhelmed by all of the needs that are evident when we look at our communities, our cities, our country and beyond. Of course, we do not have to go to the farthest parts of the world and into the fire of tragedy or grief-stricken lands. We simply need to notice what triggers our pain, what is so extremely difficult for us to tolerate that we are compelled to take action to address it. When we direct some of our attention, even in the midst of our busy lives, to getting involved and giving of ourselves, we will be guided accordingly. Often we feel compelled to start in a small way, perhaps even just by infusing more love in our daily interactions with others. If we sincerely intend to further expand our generosity, a widening flow of opportunity will naturally invite us to become part of something larger, perhaps more far-reaching. Paradoxically, when we are involved in something greater than ourselves, as shown by the stories in this book, we become at once more humble and more fulfilled. We become elevated on the wings of an expanded courage released through the spirit of our generativity.

As the path to passionate fulfillment intersects with that of self-realization, I now invite you, through the next chapter, to engage in the imperative of introspection. There, fresh insights coming to the fore may help you reach new depths of unconditional love and acceptance for yourself and others. While you expand your relationship with your authentic self, and revitalize and shift your life accordingly, you will enable your heart to sing. As you do so, you add your unique voice to those of past visionary leaders and lead your own legacy.

Questions to ponder

- What are you most grateful for in your life right now?
- How can you contribute to shaping our culture into one that fosters generosity?
- What social or ecological problem among humans or the natural world causes you the most distress or concern at this time and why?
- What beliefs do you hold about your ability to make a contribution toward the betterment of society or the environment?
- How has the call of generativity manifested in you so far in your life?

CHAPTER 5

The Homecoming Journey

Everything that happens to you is your teacher. . . .
The secret is to learn to sit at the feet of your
own life and be taught by it.

—Polly Berends

Learning to sit at the feet of our life is an inviting metaphor emphasizing the importance of making time for reflection and introspection in the hectic pace of our modern day. It encourages us to develop practices that help us to restore our connectedness with our authentic self, our soul, so that we can better heed the voice within. Only then are we poised to integrate the lessons of our own life (as teacher) and to orient ourselves toward meaningful re-engagement while traversing the middle passage or eldership.

The twenty-first-century context for the journey of midlife is that our personal evolution is intimately connected to our collective evolution. To the extent that we continue to restore the wholeness within and contribute our expanded potential, we augment the possibility of restoring wholeness in our world at this eleventh hour. This chapter invites you to heal any inner dividedness you may feel, liberate the voice of truth within, and be guided by your inner compass to make foundational, creative choices for your life. The poem that follows, by the award-winning poet Derek Walcott, poignantly captures the universal longing to come home to ourselves.

LOVE AFTER LOVE

The time will come
when, with elation
you will greet yourself arriving
at your own door, in your own mirror
and each will smile at the other's welcome,

and say, sit here. Eat.
You will love again the stranger who was your self.
Give wine. Give bread. Give back your heart
to itself, to the stranger who has loved you

all your life, whom you ignored
for another, who knows you by heart.
Take down the love letters from the bookshelf,

the photographs, the desperate notes,
peel your own image from the mirror.
Sit. Feast on your life.

Delighting in this poem brings up the memory of meeting David, a musician who, in his seventies, discovered the power of metaphors through poetry. While we talked intensely about our favorite poems, I spoke the first line of this one, "The time will come when . . ." "Aaahhhh!" he exclaimed wide-eyed, awe-stricken as he recalled the revelation triggered in him by this poem. He shared that it had changed his life by helping him to heal the deep scission within himself. "For most of my life," he said, "I have felt as if two people who intensely hated each other were at war inside me."

His words bring to mind another poet's words, T.S. Eliot's line, "Hell is the place where nothing connects." As David explained, it is hellishly painful to feel disconnected from one's own source of love, wisdom and peace. This is the hell in which he felt trapped as he experienced the presence of two opposing people within him for most of his life. Resolution of this inner conflict has taken time, but now David says, "I have really experienced the miraculous healing of the two people in me." The powerful imagery and metaphors of Walcott's poem provided a doorway through which David could enter and begin to make peace with himself. As he was healing the dividedness within, he was finally coming home to the core of his being, where peace is ever present.

What does the call to "Give back your heart to itself" evoke in you? It stirs in me the desire to more fully and consistently accept myself completely and love myself unconditionally. It reminds me that each moment provides the chance to free myself from the burden of self-judgments that I still, sometimes, place on myself. Many of us learned during our early years that acceptance and love from others were conditional on good, deserving behavior that conformed to the expectations of our parents and then our teachers. Then, in adulthood and in midlife, we are constantly exposed to the media messages urging us to be more accomplished, more successful, richer, fitter, and more youthful looking. Now, many of us are unaware of our ingrained habit of withholding love and acceptance from ourselves until we have met our own conditions and expectations. And when we have achieved something significant, we are likely to find another reason to refrain from fully owning our gifts and strengths. The messages we have internalized as self-judgments often become barriers preventing us from unleashing our greatness, giving back our "heart to itself" and "feasting" on our life.

Journeying home in treacherous times

During the 1960s and 1970s, a surge of personal development captivated our mind and our attention. For some of us, the integration of that growth led to more conscious, purposeful living, to new levels of creativity and success while doing what we love. Others drifted into various degrees of mediocrity, living by default rather than by intentional choice. Still others were driven to achieve conventional success mobilized by a quest for status and economically driven values.

In the past few years, much of the thrust in personal development has been oriented toward the acquisition of wealth. No doubt you have witnessed the abundance of programs, books and other materials designed to help people develop a "millionaire mind." The marketing for these programs is very seductive, persuading people that "making money" is the direct route to happiness.

After years of focusing on self, some boomers have become entrenched in an individualistic mindset and are still lacking in spiritual maturity, wisdom and self-acceptance. Typically, these people achieved new realizations in their personal growth processes, then retreated into their habitual, defended ways. In so doing, some have gradually slipped into a narrow scope of awareness, tossed around by life's circumstances while being unconsciously influenced by their past conditioning and their childhood's unfinished business. In these boomers, the vigilant inner self-critic is always eager to feed into doubts of not being good enough, rich enough, beautiful enough, and so on. When we are under the unconscious influence of our conditioning, we typically live on automatic pilot in a reactive, semi-conscious state.

But as James Hollis warns us in *The Middle Passage*, the longer one remains unconscious, which is easy to do in our culture, the more likely one is to see life as a meaningless succession of moments leading toward some vague end. Hollis writes "when one is stunned into consciousness, a vertical dimension intersects the horizontal plane of life; one's life span is rendered in a depth perspective." Sometimes, a critical illness or the loss of a loved one can shock a person into greater consciousness. But in midlife, we are wise to initiate our awakening and become more introspective if we have not already done so. Otherwise, circumstances, perhaps even crises of sorts, may intensify in our lives, thereby providing an auspicious time to, in Polly Berends's words, "sit at the feet of [our] own life and be taught by it."

Recovering wholeness

Typically, the yearning for greater wholeness and connectivity creates pressure on the inner barriers to self-love alluded to at the start of this chapter. To heal our dividedness, in midlife especially, we must mature enough to see ourselves as part of an interdependent web that includes the people in our family of origin and even our ancestors. As we do so we can better embrace our wholeness and reclaim or create a new place in our ancestral line as well as in the world.

The middle passage demands that we unlearn the patterns of self-judgment we have adopted and also release others whom we may have walled off with our judgments. In my personal life and professional work, I have seen that when people attempt to protect themselves from a painful past by avoiding certain family members, they are not free. What is clear to me is that the parts of others we dislike are usually aspects of ourselves that we deny. When we harbor negativity and feelings of self-loathing, we tend to project undesirable parts of ourselves that we unconsciously disown. This is how enemies are created: we see others through filters that are tinted with our own shades of darkness; we blame them and turn them into "the bad guy." In the end, the more parts of ourselves we have walled off and projected onto others, the more our heart is constricted in its flow of love and acceptance for self and others. On a much larger collective level, this is part of the downward slide that leads to warfare.

The leading German therapist Bert Hellinger stated, in an article published by Ode Magazine, that paradoxically "only when you can embrace others in your hearts are you free of them." In his work with families, Hellinger has witnessed time and again that when some family members are excluded or rejected for whatever reasons, a gap is created in the energetic field of the greater collective consciousness of the family across generations. This can lead to the emergence of an unconscious pattern or entanglement in which a person of a subsequent generation may, for example, unconsciously bond with the rejected family member, carry their guilt and take on the role of the ostracized member. Through the process of Family Constellation healing sessions, these systemic entanglements are revealed. Participants get to see, in their family system, represented by other participants, where love has flowed and where it has been cut off, causing pain and suffering, often over many generations.

I experienced this transformative work personally during a Family Healing Constellation weekend facilitated by Claudia Pétursson in Seattle, Washington. Although over the years I had healed many wounds from my past, in this Constellation, I gained more understanding of how some of my father's negative emotions had affected me. Below the layers of my pain, I saw that my father's anger had prevented me from moving with my natural exuberance and curiosity toward what I wanted as a child. And by forbidding me to express my own discontent in response to his anger, he had effectively severed my own healthy impulse of assertion, the fuel that serves to mobilize us to get our needs met and to "go for" what we want in life. Without this inner spark, we risk becoming overly passive, being too conciliatory or adopting a victim mentality.

During that healing session in Seattle, I felt an inner shift from integrating my new insights and releasing suppressed emotions associated with them. Then, I suddenly felt compassion after seeing how difficult it must have been for my father to lose between the ages of thirteen and eighteen, his father, his sister and then his mother, to illnesses. I also realized that in my unconscious loyalty toward my mother, I too had continued to suffer from the anger patterns of the men in my life, especially my ex-husband. In the last moments of the session, those representing my family system were standing in truth, in a triangle formation, a flow of warm caring emanating from them while I stood before them. When Claudia asked me to turn toward my future with my ancestors behind me, I felt their surge of loving support rushing through me for the first time in my life, causing tears to flow down my cheeks. I had found some acceptance of my past story while at the same time transforming it with my expanded insights and releasing its hold on me.

To really *live forward* on our life path, it is important that we understand and free ourselves from the old story we created in our mind during our past. This enables us to access more inner peace with those we may have previously excluded from our hearts. Then we can find ourselves anew in the network of interrelatedness that holds us together through our challenges and our victories.

Our relationship with the world and the Grand Will

How we perceive ourselves in relation to others and to our circumstances largely determines where we position ourselves on the spectrum of reactive to creative attitudes and orientations. In *The Fifth Discipline Fieldbook*, Peter Senge describes three attitudinal orientations that define how people see themselves relative to others and to outer circumstances: those with a "reactive orientation"; those with a "creative orientation"; and those with an "interdependent orientation." "The world is happening to me" is an inner view in which one's sense of control over one's life is perceived to be mostly outside of oneself. Those with this viewpoint tend to feel as though they are at the mercy of outside forces and events. This orientation is common in those who have relatively low self-esteem and are unaware of how they use their personal power indirectly, often through passive aggression, for example. Because they operate in a reactive or defensive mode, they often crave being "left alone" when confronted with requests that they tend to perceive as impositions or demands. You might know people who are oriented this way; they repeatedly perceive themselves as powerless victims of their circumstances.

On the other hand, people with a "creative orientation" tend to feel in charge of their life and their achievements. This orientation is part of the culture and language of the human potential movement. In the workplace, organizations that strongly promote this orientation may encourage employees to become workaholics while urging them to "do what it takes" to achieve their goals and to advance the company. On the extreme end of the creative spectrum, this approach can fail to acknowledge the human frailties and challenges we are all subject to as part of being human in a network of relationships.

In contrast to this, points out Senge in *The Fifth Discipline Fieldbook*, the "interdependent" orientation is one in which people see themselves as part of a greater whole. While such people strive to exercise a sense of personal mastery in their life, they are also conscious of the many factors and forces interacting both within and outside of them. People with this orientation build on their strengths, learn from their mistakes and accept the limitations that are part of the human condition.

In his book *The Path of Least Resistance: Learning to Become the Creative Force in Your Own Life*, Robert Fritz writes in depth about the creative orientation. While reading *Creating*, also by Robert Fritz, I benefited from learning about the inner dynamics of the creative process and the principles of creating. In fact I have integrated some of this understanding in my personal and professional life. However, on the spectrum from reactive to interdependent orientation, I situate myself between the creative orientation and the interdependent orientation because of my acute awareness of the relational systems influencing us all. As Martin Luther King Jr. reminded us "we are all caught in an inescapable network of mutuality, tied in a single garment of destiny. Whatever affects one directly, affects all indirectly." Like him, many other leaders were also creators of their own visions while they harnessed their soul force and the Grand Will to fulfill their mission.

We become most fulfilled when our willpower is not manipulated by self-imposed conditioning, but rather engaged in the service of our soul and the common good. And when we are deeply involved with life in this way, we are naturally drawn into alignment with the Grand Will, the universal source of life energy. The image of a tandem bicycle comes to mind as a metaphor, in which my authentic self leads the way into an expansive purpose, fueled by the passions and drive emerging from my soul in intimate connection with the Grand Will.

Developing the flow, ease and fulfillment that arise when our individual will is in dynamic, synergistic relationship with the Grand Will is nothing less than a lifelong learning journey. To the extent that we cultivate greater awareness and transcend our conditioned responses, we gain more freedom while more vitality arises through the conduits of our free will. Then we begin to notice the emergence of a creative flow, of more aliveness, of circumstances and people coming to us in convergence toward our most heartfelt endeavors. Furthermore, the confluence of circumstances and synchronicity intensifies when we strive to accomplish something that also serves the best interests of others and the common good.

Past significant events as clues to one's calling

In chapter 2, I mentioned a childhood event that became for me a significant moment, a signpost of my life's current purpose. At six years old in my classroom I was the only one to stay seated to signal my displeasure at attending school. The principal asked me again if I really meant that I did not like coming to school. Filled with a vague sense of embarrassment, I confirmed that indeed I did not like school, but I could not explain why. Eager to learn as I was then, I now know that I disliked being there largely because of the harsh disciplinarian style of the teacher. I also sensed unspoken assumptions in her interactions with students that children's ideas and opinions were neither important nor valid. Yet I knew deep down that "truth comes out of the mouth of babes," as the saying goes.

Upon my return home from school that day, I approached my mother and with innocence in my eyes, told her what had happened in the classroom. To my sorrowful surprise, my mother scolded me as she expressed her disapproval of what I had done to communicate my truth. She explained in a harsh tone of voice that my behavior would have caused an embarrassment for the teacher. In my child's mind, being scolded represented a painful injustice; I was expected to betray my feelings and pretend to like school to promote a positive impression of the teacher in the principal's eye. As an adult, I later realized that my mother meant to be protective of me; not wanting me to feel embarrassed by standing out from my peers.

Thinking back on this incident, I see my staying seated as a first expression of my desire to step out of conformity to make a statement and reveal my verity. Through this experience a seed of determination emerged in my subconscious mind. From the sense of injustice associated with this, I now recognize that germinating in me was a foundational decision to live in accordance with my truth from that moment onward. As an adult, freeing the voice of truth within me has taken on a broader, more expansive meaning. But even as a child, I sensed that conforming instead of stating my truth was too great a price to pay. Much later, my conviction was confirmed when I learned about the far-reaching impact being true to oneself can have. You will read the results of research about living truthfully in chapter 8, on wellness. And history is filled with groundbreaking moments in which truth was released and effectively shifted fundamental paradigms in people's minds.

Excavating the authentic self

Throughout our childhood most of us unconsciously adopted behavioral patterns that helped to foster a sense of belonging and relative acceptance from others. However, some of these patterns, such as telling "white lies" to be polite or hide our real feelings, contribute to a sort of inner dividedness that comes to haunt us later in life. This kind of alienation from true self is supported and encouraged through the subtleties and sayings in our language. We are told, "Don't wear your heart on your sleeve" because being transparent and open-hearted is seen as an indicator of naïveté and vulnerability. In his book *A Hidden Wholeness*, Parker Palmer explores with great eloquence and clarity the cultural roots of our dividedness. Parker points out that while being socialized to conform, many of us have been dispossessed of our gifts and our built-in inner guidance. Every time we made decisions in discord with that inner small voice, we also took steps away from our true self, thus reinforcing the pain of our dividedness.

> *What is the source of our first suffering? It lies in the*
> *fact that we hesitated to speak. It was born in the moment*
> *when we accumulated silent things within us.*
> — GASTON BACHELARD

Looking back at my early years from adulthood, I have recognized the unspoken and overt pressures that influenced me to "accumulate silent things within." As you reflect on your own life, you might also find clues to something within that is now calling to be expressed, transformed and released. But often, the pain entwined with the "silent things" is covered by layers of anger and even rage seething deep inside. In our culture it can still be difficult, for women in particular, to acknowledge, feel and release these intense emotions suppressed within. Through her empowering book *Healing Rage: Women Making Inner Peace Possible*, Ruth King helps women to stop contributing to their own suffering. Describing the six common disguises of rage, King reveals how we tend to deceive ourselves and others about our underlying shades of rage. A captivating speaker, Ruth King also leads transformative workshops and retreats to help both men and women improve their self-awareness, increase their emotional literacy and harness the transformative power of rage. Her organization, Bridges, Branches & Braids, is listed in the resources section.

In my own work with groups and individuals, I also support others to change their relationship with the "silent things within." Indeed, through introspective, even creative and expressive practices, we can "pour out" these truths. Rather than letting them out by blaming, shaming or with explosive anger, we can positively transform these things as the process of alchemy transmutes base metals into gold. This word, "alchemy," has origins in the Greek word *khymatos*, "that which is poured out." Imagine for a moment that as you transmute these painful truths, they dissipate into gold dust, illuminating the path before you. When you embrace your own truth more fully, you also help others to free themselves from the suffering caused by their own "accumulated silent things."

Often, through midlife, the quest for deeper meaning and authenticity presents itself differently for women than for men. Looking to better align who they are with what they do, women may yearn to immerse themselves in new endeavors beyond the multiple roles that have absorbed their energies so far. Depending on how much time and energy they have devoted to caring for others, midlife may prompt them to give *themselves* the space, the love, to nurture their authentic self into fuller expression. When women enter their fifties, they frequently experience, as I did, a surge of energy manifesting as a quest and a drive to move into sharply focused actions. But given the current trend of women having children into their late thirties and early forties, mothering roles may clash with midlife restlessness, the quest for more expansive meaning or for newly stimulating endeavors. Having had my second child at forty years of age, I recall being frustrated when my then two-year-old daughter Natasha had a tantrum because I had failed to cut her apple in the particular way she had tried to explain. Although I remained patient, it was difficult for me to be empathetic in these moments, because I craved to entertain much more profound, significant conversations.

Many women in their fifties also undergo difficult times brought on by the physiological symptoms of menopause. Others may feel the pain of letting go of their grown children or the grief of the "empty nest syndrome" reverberating within, prompting a search to fill the void. Appropriate responses to this transitional phase include restoring or deepening friendships, developing practices conducive to introspection, and perhaps rekindling a creative flame. Along with creativity, as they approach the threshold of eldership, women also tend to experience the emergence of deeper intuitive guidance. Embracing these energies in a balance of self-care and social contribution helps us to know ourselves beyond the nurturing roles that may have dominated our lives. For both men and women, the homecoming journey is one of restoring a deep connection with the soul and learning to better utilize its powerful energy source.

In his book *Care of the Soul*, Thomas Moore warns that when the "soul is neglected it does not just go away; it appears symptomatically in obsessions, addictions, violence, and loss of meaning." Such symptoms lead some people to feel fraudulent, because they know that the image of being successful and happy they present to the world is not authentic. Deep within they sense that real success includes living and working, with integrity, at what they most love to do and are best at.

Paul's midlife journey

In one of my professional roles—as a life transitions coach—I regularly help clients who seek to create a better alignment between who they are and what they do. One of my clients, whom I will call Paul, was reaching a midlife point of feeling in discord with himself. Having built a very successful law practice over twenty years, Paul had achieved all of the status and financial security he had so longed for as a child. He had been raised in a family of modest socio-economic means and remembers feeling a persistent embarrassment about this throughout his youth. After a few years of aimless wandering in his early twenties he began a relationship with a woman who was determined to develop an impressive career as a lawyer. The two were married and he followed her into law school.

Paul recalled that he intensely disliked his course of study in law, but he managed to convince himself that he had to get through it to reach the kind of status he so wanted. With determination fueled by a deep-seated drive for financial success, Paul had reached the top of his career at fifty years of age. But now, he was noticing that he was intensely dissatisfied with practicing law. I recall the poignant moment when he said "I feel lost," adding that he had been feeling this way for a couple of years and the feeling had become intolerable.

During the coaching process, Paul acknowledged his unbearable restlessness. He craved new challenges, wanted to recover his passions, and was tempted to stop practicing law. In the small city in which he operated and resided, he was perceived by the community as having achieved what most of us think we want: financial success, status, security, strong family bonds. In his words: "I have it all." Except that Paul realized he did not "have" himself, his wholeness. A sense of exhaustion and restlessness had intensified after years of trying to convince himself that he was enjoying his work and that all was well. Paul was now suffocating in the narrow confines of his habits, on automatic pilot yet going nowhere he really wanted to be. Hence, the persistent feeling of being lost prevailed. It was as if the voice of his authentic self had "checked out" after having been repressed and ignored repeatedly for years.

Gradually, Paul saw that the edifice of success and status he had built was now oppressing him with heavy responsibilities and demands without offering real fulfillment. In the process of shielding himself from vulnerability and the fear of financial strain, he had exerted such will and control upon himself that he had extinguished any real aliveness or creative impulses from his life. Paul was now clearly seeing that he had made major life choices based on fears of scarcity.

Tormented as he was, Paul did not really know how to reconnect with his estranged authentic self. He wanted desperately to find some new career to jump into, thinking that this would quiet his inner turmoil. Yet, after so many years building his law practice, he realized that he could not simply run away from it. As we worked together, he came to understand that a purposeful vocation, one that yields fulfillment, finds expression foremost from who we *are*, our true self. And that self is formed from our values, principles, passions, natural abilities and talents. Paul got to see that the urgent priority for him was not so much to figure out what to *do* but firstly to discover how to *be* the authentic, whole man he was yearning to be. Jumping into another career without first reconnecting with his true self for inner guidance would not likely lead to the fulfillment he sought.

Paul realized that he could no longer keep going solely driven by efforts of will. During coaching sessions, I asked him powerful questions that led him to become more introspective. He saw that to sustain himself in new, more passionate endeavors, he would have to first reconnect with the creative life force that was waiting to surge through him again. Empowered by our work in sessions, he is releasing the "silent things within" and reclaiming his gifts: the talent and passion for writing that he left behind in his early twenties. With the fresh perspective afforded by greater self-awareness, and the renewed vitality gained from permitting himself to do more of what he loves, Paul is gradually rearranging his life. He is also developing a creative orientation to life, taking courses to embrace his talents, practicing yoga regularly, and deepening his spirituality to better tap the well of wisdom within him.

From self-actualization to a mission-driven life

I think we all have a little voice inside us that will guide us. . . .
If we shut out all the noise and clutter from our lives and
listen to that voice, it will tell us the right thing to do.
— CHRISTOPHER REEVES

Sometimes, a deeper calling arises from a new direction or from a recurring theme that may have been dormant in the seeds of a soul mission. Inspired by Maslow's hierarchy of needs and informed by her two decades of work as a coaching consultant, Andrea Jacques, founder of Kyosei Consulting International, has created a new model for understanding how we grow toward a mission-driven life. Her model shows the movement forward from survival needs to thriving in integrity as we increasingly focus our lives on what matters most, what is highest in us.

The four levels of needs she has identified begin with the needs to survive and be secure, to satisfy our basic requirements for life. Then we move toward the needs associated with striving for self-esteem through skill building, achievements and gaining confidence. At the third level and beyond, our needs tend to become internally driven and other-focused rather than externally driven and self-focused. At this stage, we typically seek to feel more alive through the uniqueness of our creativity while striving to achieve excellence and greater congruence between our work and personal lives.

At the top of the pyramid, which often coincides with midlife or early eldership, our need is to thrive through the integration of all that we are and do. As we assume the mantle of leadership, particularly in innovative ways, we are filled with new surges of vitality and become better able to influence others in positive ways that are in the best interests of the common good. The following story provides the example of a man who turned within to listen to the voice of his soul and reinvent himself in midlife to be of service to nature and humanity. But unlike Paul, this man started his introspective search from being fulfilled in his personal and professional life.

I met Larry Robinson at the Quest for Global Healing conference in Bali in May 2006. Since that time, he has become a friend, a mentor and a colleague in activism. When I asked him about his midlife transitions, Larry talked about the difficult but fruitful path that he walked shortly after celebrating his fiftieth birthday in the joyful presence of friends and loved ones.

In the months that followed his birthday, Larry noticed that his enthusiasm for life was diminishing. Grateful for having a wonderful life partner, a thriving psychotherapy practice, and a rich inner life, Larry was puzzled by the intensity of the darkness that descended upon him. How could he feel so depressed while knowing that his life was filled with the blessings of a lovely partner, numerous satisfied clients, radiant health and more than sufficient material comforts? Yet, as deep as his gratitude was for his personal blessings, his despair was equally deep about the state of deterioration in the outer world and Mother Earth. How could he even begin to address complex, seemingly unsolvable problems destroying the natural world and threatening the survival of the human race?

While he spent considerable time in introspection and meditation, allowing the process to take its course, Larry remained in despair and depression for a few months. Then, one day, the voice within revealed his new calling along with a specific course of action. Larry heard loud and clear that he was to participate in the civic elections of his city in Sebastopol, California. At first, this was not an idea that he was fond of. And what if he were to fail rather than win? But the voice told him that he just had to run in the elections and be detached from the outcome. Once Larry made the commitment to heed the voice within, his depression dissipated and a new level of energy and light-heartedness infused his being.

Knowing that he had to heed the voice of the Grand Will speaking through this new calling, Larry began to research what it would take to become a city councilor. He spoke to many people who were involved in local politics and gained a greater understanding of the processes and the issues. Gradually, he saw how he could develop his stance from the strengths of his caring for his community and his ecologically driven passions. With momentous energy, Larry presented himself in the civic elections and was elected as a councilor. He has also served as the mayor of Sebastopol for two one-year terms in the past few years.

At first, Larry worked long hours to maintain his psychotherapy practice while also being devoted to local politics. But then, circumstances around him provided a new opportunity; the real estate market made a significant jump, enabling Larry to sell one his properties, invest wisely and retire, without financial concerns, from his role as a therapist.

In his third term as a city councilor now in 2008, Larry finds that daily challenges abound in his new vocation. But he knows from a sense of deep-seated contentment that this is the life he is meant to lead at this time. This work enables him to embrace his calling, to bring the power of wisdom and spirituality into the political arena as he contributes his leadership to civic governance and toward a more sustainable world. Part of what has enabled Larry to be successful in giving of himself in this role is that he truly integrated what he received from others while honing his skills, his wisdom and his ability to elicit trust.

Upon hearing about Larry's experience, especially the initial period of "not knowing" he went through, I was struck by the seemingly inner contradiction he experienced during that time. He felt an inward dividedness, at once being deeply blessed in his personal life and profoundly distressed by the despair he was feeling about the world. Because of Larry's ability to contain the ambiguity of these opposing feelings, and to listen quietly within, the tension between them dissipated as clarity rose to the surface of his mind. To use the metaphor of a pond, when the surface of the water is free of agitation or movement, it can provide a mirror effect, reflecting clearly its surroundings. From the clarity arising in Larry's mind and heart emerged a new, expansive vision of how he was to express his sense of personal mission and commitment to meaningful action. Thinking back about this passage in his life, Larry emphasizes that he has learned about the importance of maintaining a strong connection to his soul and listening to the promptings of that voice within.

Larry is also an exquisite poet, and this poem that he wrote is one of my favorites.

SNOWFLAKES

Ecclesiastes says "for everything there is a season."
You say "It's tax season;
it's baseball season; it's allergy season;
I've got to season the steak on the barbie;
besides, I don't have time to change the world."

Goethe tells us of the genius, power and magic in boldness.
You say "What can I do, anyway?
The foxes are guarding the henhouse;
the juggernaut is out of control;
we're all just snowflakes in a windstorm."

The mountain asks "Which snowflake, falling,
will be the one to send down the avalanche
to change this entire landscape?"

Through the examples of Larry's and Paul's trajectories, you can see that there are no easily followed road maps for the homecoming journey. There are numerous tools, practices and processes, including meditation, retreats, vision quests and coaching, all of which can facilitate the process of coming home to your true, more congruent self. Signposts and additional guidance are offered in chapter 14, and inspirational books and resources are listed in the resources section at the end of this book.

As you may have noticed, in the mythical quest stories that have been told through time, a common theme is that of coming back to the heart of what was there all along. This transformative process yields the ability to see everything with new eyes. Through this quest, which includes meeting layers of darkness, we ultimately reach the paradox of surrendering our ego-driven smallness while accessing our divine greatness. This is how Gandhi, Mother Teresa and Martin Luther King Jr. were able to achieve their grand and wondrous contributions to humanity.

Addressing the transition from midlife into eldership, the next section introduces you to crucial considerations in the process of orienting yourself toward a joyful re-engagement rather than an eventual *retirement*.

Questions to ponder

- What do you perceive may make it difficult for you to fully give back your heart to itself?
- Have you "accumulated silent things within" you and if so, what are they? Can you identify what these things are?

- Where do you see yourself on Senge's spectrum of attitudinal orientations, from reactive to creative to interdependent?
- How could you become more present to your life and experience it as a "feast"?
- What kind of practices, rituals, relationships or habits could you further develop to help you recover or better align with your authentic self?

Re-engagement
Not Retirement

CHAPTER 6

Freedom, Identity and Purpose

Purpose is the place where your deep
gladness meets the world's needs.

—Frederick Buechner

Those who have mostly endured rather than enjoyed their work can hardly wait to be free from the promptings of the alarm clock, from time pressures or from some co-workers. Even when our work meets our criteria of satisfaction, we still often feel constrained by the hectic pace, the rush hour traffic or the problems we have to solve daily. While many in our generation do not plan to retire in a formal way, some look forward to what they perceive as a new freedom awaiting in the gateway of eldership. In advertisement from financial planners, the word "freedom" often appears as the ultimate reward after decades of hard work, investment and wise planning.

Of course, financial abundance and security can afford us more freedom of choice, and in chapter 11 you will read more about this while you explore your relationship with money. But if we do not cultivate inner freedom, our wealth alone cannot generate the true liberty that we long for.

What is the state of mind conducive to enjoying a real sense of freedom in midlife, retirement or re-engagement? Here I invite you to consider a much broader and deeper definition of freedom than that of having enough time and money to do what we want, when we want. I believe inner freedom truly expands when we become free from our past conditioning, our attachment to the need for more possessions or to the need for being more perfect, accomplished, wealthy and so on. And when we detach from those kinds of needs, we become freer to experience sufficiency while appreciating *quality* more than *quantity* in our life. We also become more creative and open to new experiences, thereby being better able to enjoy what presents itself in the "now." With the ability to meet the "now" as it is, without wanting to modify it according to what we think it "should" be, we can enter each moment with a detached freshness of mind and curiosity. Then we may also better choose how we respond to the present rather than react from an unconsciously conditioned mindset.

In his classic work entitled *Man's Search for Meaning*, the author and psychiatrist Viktor E. Frankl writes in vivid detail about the experiences of prisoners, himself among them, in concentration camps including Auschwitz. After prisoners experienced and observed acts of unspeakable inhumanity, and were stripped of everything, Frankl still concludes that the last of the human freedoms could not be taken away; the freedom "to choose one's attitude in any given set of circumstances, to choose one's own way." In this book, Frankl states that "the men who allowed their inner hold on their moral and spiritual selves to subside eventually fell victim to the camp's degenerating influences." Frankl's profound reflections on people's way of being in such extreme adversity prove that real freedom is something that emanates from within.

By the end of midlife, entering eldership, spiritual maturity also helps us to gain more inner freedom as we become better able to tolerate ambiguity. Rather than having to classify things as good or bad, black or white, we are increasingly comfortable perceiving situations and people in the wide spectrum between black *and* white. This enables us to free ourselves from our continuing, perhaps unexamined, habits of living, thinking and the stories we make up in our minds. When we change our relationship with our thoughts, by observing or questioning at least some of them, rather than identifying with them or believing them to be true, we reach deeper levels of freedom. If we refrain from "buying into" everything that goes on in our minds, we gain the freedom to choose more of our thoughts and attitudes. In turn, this positive choice provides access to inner states and emotions that are conducive to experiencing more wellness, joy and gratitude for what we have.

Given that the nature and wisdom of the soul is often expressed in paradoxes, we may actually end up with fewer choices as we become increasingly self-aware and more conscious. The author David Whyte has said that in life we make many choices and then, once we know ourselves and deeply commit to that authenticity, we have fewer choices. What he means is that we become intensely interested and invigorated by following our inner calling as that voice guides us with increasing volume and intensity. When we heed that voice to contribute to a greater purpose and tap the creative life force within, we also free our identity from its entanglement with our possessions or our professional role.

In *Crossing the Unknown Sea: Work as a Pilgrimage of Identity*, Whyte reminds us that when we consciously involve our heart and soul in our work, it becomes like a pilgrimage, a journey with a much greater significance than just "paying the bills." Viewed this way, work can be a mutual interchange of engaging energies in which we learn about ourselves and our true purpose through our work's evolution.

One of the professionals I met while researching this book was a Vancouver dentist unusually devoted to his work and his patients. Donald Marshall's way of practicing dentistry was remarkably holistic, kind and attentive. I conversed with him a few months after he retired, in his early seventies. I heard that at his retirement party, hundreds of patients were present and many lined up to speak about their experience of Dr. Marshall. One person even said, "I finally figured out what it was that he was injecting me with all of those years right along with the freezing substance. . . . It was love." Here is an example of practicing one's profession with wholeheartedness and within a greater purpose which is, ultimately, the "real work" of "injecting" love into others through what we do.

Don Marshall is now using his retirement to explore his creativity, devote more time to his wife Diane and their grandchildren, travel to visit friends, take courses at university and volunteer in his community. He continues to attend deeply to his inner life, and can better appreciate life and nature without the time constraints previously imposed by his practice. Dr. Marshall transitioned into retirement with relative ease as a result of the personal congruence, deep satisfaction and integrity with which he worked and helped people as an exceptional dentist. Yet, having been attuned to his spiritual essence throughout his life, Dr. Marshall maintained his true sense of personal identity as distinct from his professional role.

Restoring your personal identity

Upon entering retirement, if you have been overly consumed by your professional role while unknowingly neglecting your personal life, you will need to reacquaint yourself with, in the words of Derek Walcott, "the stranger who was your self." Whether or not you have been intensely focused on achieving status and or financial wealth, you may be asking yourself, "What will I do?" Yet very few people contemplate the question *Who will I be?* when they approach this transition. Our culture supports this off-balance emphasis on *doing* at the expense of identifying the values and qualities of *being* we want to inhabit and bring forward with our actions. We are used to shaping our identities according to our roles and titles, what we *do*. This is reflected in the way we introduce ourselves in response to the question "What do you *do*?" We typically respond by saying "I *am* a . . . ," thus reinforcing the misperception that we are our professional role.

Some high-stress all-consuming professions require such intense dedication that maintaining a balanced relationship with yourself and with others can be very difficult. When I interviewed an officer from the Royal Canadian Mounted Police, for example, I learned that most officers have difficulty finding time and energy to adequately attend to their personal life or pursue their own interests. Upon retirement re-entering their own personal life, it is as if they are walking into a foreign country; they realize how estranged from themselves they have become. Furthermore, since their working environment is a place to which they feel they belong, retirement triggers fears of being lost and alienated. For such individuals, rebuilding one's identity and renewing one's sense of purpose becomes an utmost priority. Current statistics show a high rate of early death among those who opt for a full retirement from this type of work without having engaged in the necessary transition process. Unfortunately, aside from financial planning advice, few opportunities are currently provided to help people in such professions gradually reorient themselves for a smooth transition into retirement.

Perhaps you are among those who have been part of a work environment that resembles a heated cauldron of competitiveness and even greed-driven values. In such workplaces, we are often subtly and persistently influenced by the cultural messages that emanate from the organization we represent and even, to various degrees, identify with. This also makes it more difficult for us to discern who we really are and determine the nature of the moral fiber we are made of. Yet, as stated in chapter 5, every time we ignore our own truth and values, we betray ourselves and become further estranged from self.

Among executives in the business world, retirement can mean the loss of high status and the corporate image that, over decades, they have come to see as part of themselves. Some executive once said that retirement is a four-letter word. He explained, "That's when you go from introducing yourself as who's who to who's that." In the corporate world and even, sometimes, among professionals, years of energy are invested to build an image of being "somebody."

Sometimes, that "somebody" is built in an attempt to counteract a deep-seated sense of unworthiness. Or, as in the case of Paul in the previous chapter, this investment in building a certain image and identity is a reactive defense to fears of financial scarcity. For others, the "somebody-ness" is appealing as an outcome of achieving status, which most of us, especially men, have been conditioned to view as a priority in our culture. In subtle ways, the influences of our culture lead us to feel most worthy when we are earning significant sums of money or when we have an impressive net worth. Intuitively, we may sense that parting with our status and earning less or no money in retirement will confront us with our deep-seated unworthiness again. Ultimately, we will only experience deepening fulfillment when we practice the art of centering our sense of identity in our spiritual essence, the source of our authentic self.

Moving forward beyond anxiety and exhaustion

Departing from a form of work we have loved for years can feel as though we are hollowing out the bone marrow at the center of our life. For those who work in an environment highly congruent with their values, leaving bonds of friendship and collaboration to retire may bring on some fears of isolation. A friend who is blessed with great working relationships and plays a leadership role in the field of child care and development shared such fears with me. When she was reminded, in a conversation, that retirement was coming up for her, she said a sense of anguish came up in her chest. Later that night, when she tried to sleep, the thought of retirement popped into her mind and triggered a surge of panic.

"I had to put the light on and read a little to calm down," she said, astonished by her reaction. She is now in the process of exploring what compels her most in her search for a renewed purpose. Perceptively, she realizes that acknowledging rather than avoiding or denying the grief of leaving her colleagues will assist in her transition. Knowing that she thrives best in a community of like-minded people, she is presently seeking options that combine community-making with the contribution of her wisdom and expertise. Eventually, most of us can learn, sometimes with needed help, that our love of our work, our skills and our talents can find other forms of expression even beyond a formal retirement.

This learning process can be facilitated by a retirement coach, who supports people in this transition to rediscover what they really need, want and aspire to at this turning point of life. Sometimes, midlife or retiring clients arrive in my coaching practice with a sense of exhaustion. I remind them that this fatigue is not only or necessarily due to being overworked. A deep tiredness may also come from having unknowingly used-up energy to suffocate the desires for change arising from our authentic self. These are the changes we crave to make in order to really live fully through doing more of what we love, such as in the example of Paul in chapter 5. Confusion is another inner dynamic that creates exhaustion. When we are feeling opposing impulses, such as to retire or not, whether to start an enterprise or not, moving elsewhere or divorcing, our energies become drained by such internal dilemma and indecisiveness. With patience, inner guidance and support from others, we can traverse the process of getting more clarity about what would truly fulfill us and then initiate the necessary changes in a timely manner.

Discovering a deeper purpose

I began to have an idea of my life, not as the slow shaping
of achievement to fit my preconceived purposes, but as the gradual
discovery and growth of a purpose which I did not know.
— JOHANNA FIELD

The quest for purposeful living is a salient theme and preoccupation among boomers—and has been for decades. For some, a primary life purpose grew as an outcome of discovering special talents, channeled into a profession to which they have given themselves. For others, a defining moment or some form of adversity triggered a deep engagement with something compelling around which they developed their work. In chapter 14, you will read more examples of satisfying and purposeful reengagement including Dr. Chandra's story of overcoming adversity.

Most often, however, there is not only one central purpose to our life. Some spiritual teachers tell us, our central purpose is to fulfill our destiny, experience joy, love others, and awaken from the illusion of our separateness from God. Our interdependent reality as humans also means that our purpose is influenced by our developmental stages and our social ecology. For example, in my late thirties I was devoted to motherhood for several years. At that time of life, my purpose to empower, inspire, educate, guide and love was expressed in my role as a parent. With my children now in their teen years, my sense of purpose is further expanding through my writing, my work with clients and service-oriented projects. For some in our generation, new caretaking responsibilities emerge when their aging parents lose degrees of independence. You will read more about relationships with those who need us in the next chapter.

As the psychologist and author of *The New Retirement* Dr. Richard Johnson affirms in his work with retirees, purpose is the fuel that feeds the fire of aliveness within. When we are devoid of purpose, the fire of aliveness may lose its brightness while our vitality subsides and our immune system is more at risk of breaking down. During midlife or on the threshold of eldership, we often feel more urgency about determining our direction into a purpose that is congruent with who we are while we redefine our personal identity. But we are wise to temper this urgency by cultivating patience with the transition process of re-engagement. Within a creative/interdependent orientation, we can practice trusting the life force within as our best teacher and guide. Just as the life force moves through the cycles of nature, we can align ourselves with that flow and allow it to guide us in the best use of our remaining decades. If you nurture a sincere desire to make a difference with your life, the power of that commitment will help reveal a purpose, a way to increase your sense of social utility, or perhaps to be of service to the natural world.

Engaging in purposeful endeavors

An increasing number of retirement-age professionals today become semi-retired as they convert their experience and skills into a part-time consultancy service. Others become mentors, work as volunteers or, as Susan Smith did, begin organizations in service of humanity. Some nearly retired people keep part-time employment in the field they have enjoyed and in which they have also become exceptionally knowledgeable. The governments of many countries have either eliminated mandatory retirement or are in the process of doing so. This enables workers' wealth of knowledge to keep benefiting organizations and helps reduce the shortage of highly experienced employees. For those who are self-employed, and nourished by their work, the concept of retirement may not even enter their mind. Yet many welcome the time when they will transfer the love of their work onto other endeavors and learning opportunities. What is important to remember here is that keeping our minds and hearts free to explore new possibilities is essential for our last few decades to be rich with engaging and exciting work or activities.

Neil Griggs is one person who has expanded the work he loved in midlife to benefit others in developing countries. Having lived in several different countries with his family as a child, Neil had developed an inquisitive mind and a great appreciation for cultural differences. In adult life, this appreciation grew into an understanding of the commonality we all share, deep down. Following a master's degree in urban planning he enjoyed a long career as a project manager. Through midlife, he started to think about how he could extend his specific skills and knowledge to help others in developing countries. His ideas came into fruition when he founded Builders Without

Borders, a Canadian registered charitable organization that has been playing a significant role in rebuilding communities since its inception in 1999.

When I met with him in Vancouver, Neil said that although his organization is primarily focused on rebuilding after disasters, keen and skilled volunteers for BWB provide other benefits to local people as well. For example, a Canadian woman had volunteered for BWB by going to Turkey and helping women in a small village to learn some carpentry skills. With these skills, these women could make some simple furniture and toys that they could sell for extra income. One of these women encountered some initial resistance from her husband, who wanted his wife to stay home and attend to homemaking tasks. Then the husband said if the broken chair in the house could be fixed, he would let her go to be trained and learn. Sure enough, the chair was fixed and the woman was later able to earn much-needed extra income through making and selling some toys and small pieces of furniture.

Neil explained that part of his satisfaction from operating this organization comes from observing that the volunteers come back changed, with broader perspectives and a new sense of gratitude. Additionally, they are more at peace with themselves, knowing that they have made a difference and that their work has an ongoing positive impact in the lives of others across the planet. For example, recently, at the end of his assignment, one of the volunteers gave his laptop to a young woman who was about to start a course of study. Neil emphasized that virtually all of the volunteers develop bonds with some of the people they get to know while working abroad. These bonds endure across the distances as the families remain in contact and the volunteers keep providing support in various ways. "That's the immeasurable impact of what people get to do through our organization," said Neil, his face glowing with satisfaction.

As our conversation came to a close, Neil's final word was "NOW." "Many people think about getting involved for too long," he said. They procrastinate or wait for the perfect circumstances to arise. "Now," insists Neil, as he makes this call to action; now is the time for people to harness their will, their skills and their desire to help and get involved. The only thing they may regret after getting started is not having done it sooner. You can read more about Builders Without Borders on their website, listed in the resources section at the end of this book.

In the summer of 2006, my search for retirees who are re-engaged into service led me to George and Beth Scott, founders of ACCES (the African Canadian Continuing Education Society). Since 1993 ACCES has been helping young Kenyans obtain the skills and education needed to benefit themselves and their society through postsecondary scholarships, primary schools, HIV/AIDS awareness, and small-business training and loans.

During a sunny afternoon in the summer of 2006, I sat with the Scotts on their oceanside lawn in White Rock, British Columbia, as they told me their post-retirement story. George had enjoyed working as a lawyer for several decades, but he did not like the poor image often associated with his profession. His wife Beth had been a teacher for many years and then a school principal. She entered retirement while she was still in her fifties, but she was not about to simply, in her words, "retire on the beach." She went on to complete her doctorate in education during the early stages of founding ACCES. As I told them about this book project, George said that, being a decade ahead of the baby boomers, he had occasionally felt envious of them. It seemed to him that the boomers' generation could benefit from a world of new opportunities as they launched themselves into careers and other exciting endeavors.

But as he entered retirement, George did not miss out on a grand opportunity to find a new purpose and give back in a truly significant way. Moving beyond his law practice, he reconnected with the best of his personal identity as a man of character with heart-driven values. In our conversation, his humility surfaced as he gave much of the credit to Beth for her steadfast ability to turn her vision into an effective course of action in the creation and operations of ACCES.

As George and Beth told me about the accomplishments of their society, I sensed that this work was, in Frederick Buechner's words, a true vocation where "deep gladness meets the world's needs." The Scotts became particularly animated as they talked about the letters of immense gratitude they often receive from students in Kenya. While they provide others the means to education, they are truly appreciative of what they have learned from Kenyans, about the strength of their human spirit, their resilience, their perseverance and their strong solidarity with each other.

"Sometimes," says George, "we're asked why we chose to address the needs of young people in Kenya rather than finding some worthy cause here in Canada. We think it's our responsibility, as citizens of an affluent country, to respond to the wants of those in developing countries." Since 1993 hundreds of children and youth have been able to access an education that is a doorway out of poverty. Through their organization, George and Beth also offer other Westerners the chance to practice their compassion-in-action and be fulfilled by the benefits of their generosity. "Occasionally, some of our donors go to Kenya to be present at the graduation of the young person they have sponsored." Naturally, this is a deeply moving experience that brings profound satisfaction. You will find a link for ACCES in the resources section.

> *History is being rewritten right now.*
> *You can stand by and watch or you can participate.*
> — BONO

The Scotts, Neil Griggs and countless others are participating in the reallocation of resources while helping to rewrite the course of history. Some of us are called into benevolent action in faraway countries while others are moved into a new purpose in the heart of our own neighborhood, as you will read in the next chapter. I invite you to consider new possibilities that can open, like a stream into a bay, in the relational fields that connect us all.

Questions to ponder

- What in your self or your life has been the basis of your personal identity?
- What, if anything, holds you back from expanding your inner sense of freedom to more fully embrace and enjoy your life as it is?
- What stands out as an experience or challenge you have learned the most from during the last twenty to thirty years of your work life?
- What part of you, perhaps creative, spiritual or otherwise, have you neglected to develop or explore while you were busy with your work life?
- If you were to identify a recurring theme, perhaps a social or ecological problem in our world, that really upsets you, what would that be?

CHAPTER 7

Relationships in Midlife and Beyond

People will forget what you said, people will forget what you did, but people will never forget how you made them feel.

—Maya Angelou

A glacial stare in the boardroom, a low blow at the staff meeting or a kind gesture in the midst of a bad day: in our working lives we have witnessed the full range of emotional reactions from co-workers. At times, the workplace resembles a downhill ride, with exhilaration rebounding in a flow of synergy. At other times, we may feel we are struggling to make our way through an obstacle course of bureaucracy or office politics. Perhaps you have experienced sabotage from a colleague or, conversely, the integrity of a co-worker speaking up to ensure that you receive your due credits. In the end, we certainly remember the kinds of emotions some people and their actions triggered in us.

Our place of work, where we invest the best of ourselves, rarely leaves us indifferent. It is where we meet the joys of fraternity and solidarity or we encounter the anguish of envy, animosity and fierce competitiveness. Whether we work primarily alone or with others, we bring so much of ourselves to work: our personal history, our fragile ego and our talents and gifts. For better or for worse, all of that becomes interwoven in a web of community that binds us to those with whom we interact in our workplace.

When we approach retirement and know that we are about to leave our colleagues behind, we may experience some degree of anxiety—even if we are welcoming our next stage of life. Those who remain employed in some part-time capacity may notice an erosion of their bonds with co-workers. Not being there on a daily basis, part-time employees are bound to miss out on some of what others go through and share together.

In response to feelings of aloneness or grief, some retirees throw themselves into a whirlwind of new activities they have long wanted to try. Sometimes, the busyness covers a deeper anxiety that is part of the initial and middle stages of transition into re-engagement. If you are yearning to hear your next calling after some form of retirement, you are wise to include quiet time in your days to listen to your inner voice. This is what Bob Scavullo of San Francisco did after he retired from a successful career in the high-tech industry a few years ago. "I took a whole summer off," said Bob, who allowed himself time to think, contemplate and assess his options.

New relationships as a source of meaning

> *Treat people as if they were what they ought to be and you*
> *help them to become what they are capable of being.*
> —JOHANN WOLFGANG VON GOETHE

When I spoke with Bob in San Francisco, he said that soon after his summer of reflection, he spoke with a few people he respected and admired, then called the principal of a nearby high school. Given his particular interest in supporting teens with special needs, Bob offered himself as a tutor. After first devoting some time to learning more about effective ways to help teenage students, he began to tutor some students in their homes and also at the school.

While he talked about his continuing involvement with the students, I could tell by the energy in his voice that Bob really enjoys his role. "Although my role is mostly about tutoring, my real job is to be a life coach and a mentor for these teens. After three or four sessions, we bond and our interactions change into a much deeper kind of conversation." Bob added that while he enjoys spending time with the students, he also rises up to the responsibility of being a role model. He particularly likes to help the teens develop the strength of their character. When we talked about the legacy he is proactively leaving, Bob said of the students he helps, "I know they'll remember me."

"When I wake up in the morning," he said, "I know there are people counting on me and that provides a great motivation." His efforts and commitment to his role as tutor and mentor have been truly appreciated in the community, and in October 2004, Bob received the school volunteer award from the mayor of San Francisco. When Bob travels through the States, he visits other high schools and speaks to others about the fulfillment he gets from helping people of this younger generation. Exemplifying the above quotation from Goethe, Bob is helping teens to become what they are capable of being.

Bringing discernment to friendships

> *Keep away from people who try to belittle your ambitions.*
> *Small people always do that, but the really great make you*
> *feel that you, too, can become great.*
> — MARK TWAIN

Among the new relationships you are drawn to develop in the second half of your life, friendships can be increasingly precious sources of companionship, joy and compassion. As part of your psychosocial and spiritual development in midlife and eldership, you may find your friendships deepening into fulfilling exchanges of mutual support. If we experience health problems as we age or lose loved ones, a trusted friend is needed to help us face our most difficult moments.

For most men, even when work and family have been the highest of priorities during their working life, retirement can stimulate a new hunger for the companionship of others of like mind. When men become less driven by economic achievements and begin to make space in their life for contemplation and reflection, they become more engaging companions. With fewer time pressures, most of us can make time for cultivating friendships that correspond to the needs we all have to be seen, heard and appreciated as we are. Many men see their wife as their one and only confidante and special friend. But it is wise to also nurture other friendships that could be nearly lifesaving in the event of the loss of one's partner or spouse. And, of course, great friendships generate a lovely synergy and make shared activities more enjoyable. In the company of those with whom we experience a generosity of heart and lightness of being, we become revitalized.

The threshold of our second life can be an opportune time to reevaluate, renew or release some of our friendships. Depending on whether you find yourself augmented or diminished in their company, you may become increasingly drawn to or repelled by certain people. Our reaction to certain people may also reveal something about our own state of mind. A friend of mine recently said that she was candidly told by another friend: "You're too happy. It makes me feel uncomfortable. I don't want you to be so happy because then I look at my life and feel that I'm not successful at getting what I really want." The paradigms that prevail in our culture can easily translate into the illusion that if someone else is happy, we will have less happiness for ourselves, as if there isn't enough to go around. We need to watch for and banish this scarcity mentality. In my experience, those with positive attitudes who focus on the greater potential in us and in themselves can become a sort of accomplice, walking an expansive path into fulfillment alongside us.

Having valued close friendships for decades, I see that, in midlife, my friends are of crucial importance while I move forward on the uncommon path I have chosen. Over time, however, the comfort of familiarity may not be sufficient to sustain the relationship. Some of my friendships have deepened and others have become obsolete because I have felt constricted by a friend's inability to expand their perception of me as I evolve. Perhaps you have also experienced decreased satisfaction in some of your friendships over time, when conversations become overly predictable or a friend maintains a kind of barrier to keep you at a certain distance. Gradually, I have moved away from such friendships in which the other appears to be mostly invested in maintaining a façade. Just like every other area of life, relationships are not static. In friendships, just as in romantic love, relationships move forward and are kept alive through various forms of attention and sharing; otherwise, they deteriorate and eventually dissipate into nothingness. When friends mutually contribute their openness and sincerity, they actively participate in the growth of a true friendship.

If you intend to live more fully, in congruence with your soul, you will gravitate towards friendships that match that way of being. A willingness to be appropriately vulnerable and be seen as we are, with our highs and lows, troubles and triumphs, generates a deeper trust that gives the friendship its satisfying richness. In the presence of such a friend, we bask in the intimacy (into-me-see) of who we are with each other, in the preciousness of our most authentic selves. Especially in this age of quick electronic exchanges and the growing anonymity of urban life, we all crave, deep down, genuine and intimate friendships. The intimacy we experience with authentic friendships helps to counterbalance the desolate aloneness that often characterizes our fast-paced modern life.

Every time you begin a relationship with a new friend, you have the opportunity to see yourself anew through the eyes of that person. In a friendly relationship, two people can create a spacious place wherein the other may roam free in joyful evolution, supported in their continuing development. Through the difficult times as well as the periods of ease, a true friend helps us ground ourselves in interconnectedness with others while we find our own inner serenity. As Goethe said so well, when we treat our friends as what they aspire to grow into, "we help them to become what they are capable of being." This kind of friendship is what the late author and poet John O'Donohue explains and celebrates in his best seller *Anam Cara*, which means "soul friend." It is a kind of friendship in which we can be truthful mirrors to each other's soul as we help one another to honor and bring to fruition the beautiful longings in our heart.

Colliding on home ground

When married couples enjoy a fulfilling relationship, there is always, at the heart of it, a special kind of friendship that keeps on nurturing them. But in midlife especially, the many responsibilities of domesticity, of work and of parenting have crowded out the place that was initially made for intimacy and friendship. At the pace of modern living, it becomes increasingly difficult for many couples to reserve the time needed to keep the flame alive, particularly after many years of marriage.

Even while equality between the sexes becomes a stronger value in our homes, the pull of biological gender-driven tendencies prevails. In many homes men help out but women are still largely in charge of orchestrating and attending to the physical, emotional and social needs of the family. Also, according to Statistics Canada, most women tend to retire a year or two earlier than men. Typically, when a woman retires, she develops new interests and renews friendships in the midst of redefining her personal identity. When women find their retired husbands occupying more space in the domestic domain they have managed for years, tensions are likely to arise. *Maclean's* magazine recently reported that women in Japan experience great difficulty adapting to the presence of their newly retired husbands in the home. According to this article, many Japanese women file for divorce shortly after their partner's retirement. This social problem is not unique to Japan.

When it comes to establishing a new identity and corresponding interests as distinct from one's previous professional role, men, in particular, as previously alluded to, may find themselves intensely challenged. Given that their self-esteem and self-worth is most often invested in their work performance and earning capacity, men typically struggle more than women to adjust to retirement. The difference in the capacity to adjust can give rise to conflicts in the home, especially when partners are retiring around the same time but adapting at a different pace. On the other hand, partners retiring at about the same time also have greater possibilities of reconnecting in a new significant purpose as George and Beth Scott did (see chapter 6). Later in this chapter, you will meet another couple who have become fulfilled together in their shared, uncommon, re-engagement.

The rising tide of divorce in midlife

With the fifty to sixty hours per week that some executives and professionals spend at work, it is not surprising they become estranged from the people in their personal life. Sometimes the distance has grown into an abyss that seems impossible to cross. We may feel a lingering yearning to connect but may not know how to. What's more, the degree of sharing and intimacy that men and women want in relationships often differs, because women are generally much more relational than men. This difference contributes to the challenging gap between them.

Even in homes where the walls have witnessed few moments of conflict or irritation, it is common to realize at the end of midlife that we do not deeply know the person by our side. After years of taking our best behaviors to work, of pouring care and attention into children—now perhaps leaving home as young adults—we may suddenly notice that our home resembles a wasteland of empty gestures. The current rise of divorce in the middle and senior years indicates that many couples arrive at this empty place, sometimes after decades of marriage, to realize that their relationship has come to an end. For couples entering retirement, such emotional distance may echo even more loudly in the hollowness created by the absence of their previous all-consuming focus on work.

In 2004, an extensive survey about divorce in midlife and beyond was undertaken by the American Association of Retired Persons. Based on the responses of 1,147 women and men aged 40 to 79, one finding was that 66 percent of women in that age range instigated divorce. According to these survey results, published in *Maclean's* magazine, the men and women who sought divorce were looking for more "freedom," a renewed "identity" and greater "fulfillment." In spite of experiencing fear before and stress after their divorce, 75 percent of those who divorced indicated that they did not regret their decision to part.

Such divorce statistics speak to our longer life expectancy and the fact that men and women are no longer satisfied uniting just out of economic necessity or to raise a family. In midlife, when the purpose of having a family has been served, some couples find it difficult to redefine the primary intent behind their continuing cohabitation. Frequently, one partner evolves, wants to shift toward a more authentic life, while the other is content to maintain habitual patterns without noticing the rift that has grown between them.

Sometimes partners feel pulled in opposing directions because their new developmental needs collide with the habitual patterns of the long-term relationship. On one hand, there's a longing to regain the intimacy that was once present. On the other hand, the yearning for change may motivate one of the partners to seek a new significant other, hoping to find more fulfill-ment in a new beginning. But if the change is initiated in reactivity, as an unconscious way to avoid taking on our developmental tasks, it is bound to lead to greater challenges and complications. Rather than facing and ad-dressing the incongruence or dissonance that surfaces in midlife, we may distract ourselves by instigating external changes. As a woman in midlife myself, I repeatedly hear women in their fifties lamenting the fact that they have been suddenly left for a younger woman. During their fifties especially, some men begin to fear mortality and seek to bind themselves to youthful women in a subconscious attempt to appease fears of aging. Meanwhile, unmarried women in midlife often feel they have much to offer, but a significant portion of men in that age range appear uninterested in partnering with middle-aged women. On the other hand, when mature people partner after each has learned from their past, a sense of ease, appreciation and respect tends to flourish, especially when partners intend to draw out the best in each other.

The price of stagnancy in marriage

During my previous years of work as a family counselor, I observed many couples who had settled into a mediocre quality of relating to which they had become accustomed. Often, such partners are entrenched in the habit of focusing primarily on what they dislike about each other, in contrast to their early romantic stage. Over time, among such partners, the weight of accumulated unfinished business and stored up resentment can create a toxic barrier that is very difficult to overcome. Metaphorically, much like clogged arteries reduce blood flow in one's body, untruths and concealment in relationships reduce emotional energy and vitality. Areas of concealment constrict communication circuits, and fewer areas of relatedness remain through which partners can connect and maintain intimate bonds. With narrower channels of connectedness, the life force, emotions (energy-in-motion) and the flow of love are eventually extinguished. Thus, the relationship becomes stagnant and potentially toxic.

In the first few years of my own marriage, we had periods of relative harmony, especially when, based on my initiative, we would spend time to talk, sort out issues and return to loving feelings. Over time, for various reasons, it was increasingly difficult for me to provide most of the energy and motivation to keep the flow of love and communication circulating in our relationship. Then after twelve years of marriage, I heard my husband say that he had "felt emotionally divorced for some time." I suddenly realized I could no longer invest most of the emotional energy in this relationship, just as it is impossible to clap with one hand. I knew that any further efforts on my part would be futile and that it was time to plan for the separation that we had started to think about. Because our two children were preteens, I worried that a separation would cause them much stress and hesitated for some time. But a year later, after the children were prepared, I initiated a separation. Like 75 percent of others who parted from their spouses in midlife, I have never regretted my decision and our children are now thriving in their teenage years.

Even at the time of separation I did not see the end of my marriage as a failure. Like many people today, my perception of marriage is not necessarily that of an enduring, permanent union "till death do us part." Every relationship has a life of its own, and a sincere mutual commitment is necessary to sustain it over an extended period of time. Sometimes, as in my case, when a marriage gradually dissolves and a grieving period follows, a new form of relationship may appear: that of being parenting partners or perhaps even just friends.

For some couples, the signs are loud and clear that it is time to allow such a transformation, or dissolution to occur. Yet some stay in unhappy marriages because the alternative can be too frightening. Remaining in the illusory safety of a marriage that resembles an old empty shell exacts a significant price; partners are drained of real vitality as they become emotionally exhausted or numb. What is more, all of the unspoken truth accumulated in such a relationship can fester within, and the toxic atmosphere that results may lead to illness. If they approach the threshold of retirement in this state, partners will have little energy available to envision or engage in new and exciting endeavors.

Casting new light on relationships

As part of the midlife transition or in the gateway to retirement, the impulse toward self-discovery may be felt as an imperative by one partner and not by the other. When this happens pressures mount and the widening gap may grow, perhaps even to the breaking point in a marriage. Sometimes, in a courageous act of self-leadership taken to embrace a calling, one partner may inspire the other toward deepening self-knowledge. Such was the case for my friend Sarah, who felt intensely drawn to undertake a long pilgrimage in Europe in the fall of 2007. In almost thirty years of marriage, Sarah's husband Roberto had consistently supported her to go where she felt she needed to be. But this time Roberto realized that Sarah would be further transformed after a journey of this magnitude, and he came to see that he wanted to be with her in this life-changing experience. So he decided to join her on this sacred pilgrimage.

Sarah and Roberto walked together on the Camino de Santiago from Saint-Jean Pied de Port in France to Santiago de Compostela in Spain: five hundred miles over thirty-two days. Through the simplest moments and the most challenging times on this pilgrimage, Sarah felt a heightened mutual caring between her and Roberto. Taking themselves out of the busy pace of their normal life and habitual patterns of relating enabled them to be more fully present and to see one another in a more authentic light. In this luminescence, they entered a new realm of vulnerability, thereby gaining a better appreciation for the courage and the simple beauty they saw in each other.

Walking side by side as pilgrims, each in their own journey, paradoxically yielded a deep sense of togetherness for Sarah and Roberto. Reflecting back on this, Sarah said this odyssey on the Camino de Santiago helped her to heal a mild lingering sense of disconnection within and to restore her relationship with the world. In so doing, she naturally embraced the yearnings in her heart to open more deeply into love—with Roberto, with others and with life itself.

In midlife we often crave a greater congruence between who we are becoming on our developmental path and how we are perceived by our partner. Sharing extraordinary experiences together, as Sarah and Roberto did, can provide that opportunity to see each other with fresh eyes. Certainly, to recover a sense of ease in continuing relationships, we must clear any discord that may be present within and that has diminished our ability to love and accept ourselves and others fully. And while we restore our inner marriage, the balance of the feminine and masculine energies within ourselves, we can become better attuned to our outer marriage. In that attunement, we learn to be more tolerant of the winds of discord and to foster harmonies of the dance that unfolds between our self and our partner. In her book *Gift from the Sea*, Anne Morrow Lindbergh eloquently captures the essence of this loving flow as she writes:

When the heart is flooded with love there is no room in it for fear, for doubt, for hesitation. And it is this lack of fear that makes for the dance. When each partner loves so completely that he has forgotten to ask himself whether or not he is loved in return; when he only knows that he loves and is moving to its music—then, and then only, are two people able to dance perfectly in tune to the same rhythm.

With a courageous fortitude, for such a renewal takes courage, each of us can practice retrieving the fears, guilt or shame that may have clouded our vision. We can relearn to see the other with the eyes of our heart rather than through the judgmental filters of our ego. In this depth of openness we can let our hearts be once again "flooded with love." This is what infuses the dance of relationship with a sense of wonder and delight. In a renewed appreciation of and enhanced quality of presence with each other, partners may experience a renewal of shared purpose along with a sense of clarity and ease. The next section gives examples of people who have enriched their primary relationships through surrendering to love together in the convergence of renewed purpose.

Relationships entwined in renewed purpose

Love does not consist in gazing at each other,
but in looking outward together in the same direction.
— ANTOINE DE SAINT-EXUPÉRY

Through the middle passage and beyond, we typically yearn to discover a new vision of shared purpose that reaches beyond care-giving or parenting roles we have taken on. I have observed an exquisite kind of complicity in couples who live and work together as they contribute to the inspired Future we all long for. Think, for example, of the collaboration between Jimmy Carter and his wife Rosalyn as they created the Habitat for Humanity following Carter's retirement. Through the strength of their synergy, experience and mutual support, they have created homes for numerous people around the world. Likewise, George and Beth Scott in British Columbia, co-founders of African Canadian Continuing Education Society, whom you met in chapter 6, have developed their union out of a shared commitment to look "outward together in the same direction."

During a trip to Italy in 2006 in which I joined a clowning tour inspired by the work of Patch Adams, I met a Japanese couple who had found a new shared purpose through the joyful activity of clowning. Having been retired for one year, Ton Chan was finally able to join his wife on frequent clowning trips. Ton said he worked in the field of medical research for more than thirty-four years at the rate of ten hours per day, and now he really enjoys allowing his inner child to come out and play.

The clowning character Ton inhabits developed gradually over the years as he joined his wife in clowning activities occasionally on weekends. With a broad smile on his face, Ton said he likes the facility with which his clowning character interacts with the children. He makes eye contact, smiles, and brings joy to children and adults alike. His wife Pei is a wonderfully spirited clown with many talents. Among them, she has developed the art of making amazingly complex animals with balloons. Together in the artistry of clowning, this couple has enhanced their connectedness through the greater purpose of sharing their compassionate hearts with people of all ages far and wide.

When new or long-time couples enter retirement with exciting projects, activities or missions before them, they at once infuse their relationship with fresh vitality. As they focus their attention on a common endeavor, partners can experience new depths of attunement and joy. Although tension can arise when the dance of give and take does not flow lightly, there is potential in such shared pursuits for each partner and the relationship itself to be greatly enriched.

The joy of grandparenting

For some couples in midlife or eldership, the joy of being grandparents becomes part of a new shared purpose. In that role, many find that they can enjoy the beauty and wonderment of childhood to a greater extent than when they were parents with multiple responsibilities. For retirees who no longer feel the typical rush associated with their work life, grandchildren can be a most cherished gift. Those who take on a caregiving role may find great satisfaction as they play a significant role in these children's lives. Others choose to cultivate strong bonds with their grandchildren through sharing various educational or recreational activities. Sometimes, a physical distance

makes it difficult for strong bonds to be maintained between extended family members. But when a significant involvement is possible, the pleasure
and satisfaction a grandparent gains from witnessing a child's development
surely adds meaning to one's life.

In the spirit of generational responsibility, some grandparents choose
to be involved in humanitarian or nature-preserving activities. With their
grandchildren in mind and heart, they find a renewed motivation to participate in some way in the betterment of our world for the generations to
come.

Relationships with those who need us

As you know, in the past twenty years, most couples have started their families increasingly late in life. Having children in their thirties and into their
forties, men and women may retire in their late fifties or early sixties with
teenagers still at home. Sometimes retirement may be postponed in order
to generate the income required to help young adult children complete their
education.

Aging parents may also require much of our attention at this stage of
our life. Often called the sandwich generation, many boomers are caught
between the needs of aging parents and those of teenagers or young adults.
And given the distance that often separates family members these days, caring for an elderly parent that may reside thousands of miles away exacer-
bates the challenges of attending to their needs and our own. The more we
can serve the needs of family without experiencing this as a burdensome
obligation, the better we will be able to maintain the positive mindset
needed to enjoy our retirement. Even when our commitments to caring for
family seem to diminish our opportunities for travel or other pursuits, we
can come to see these commitments as ultimately contributing to our growth.
After all, given current life expectancies, we will likely have many more years
to do just as we wish, after our parents have died.

One of my friends (whom I will call Sylvia) recently retired. During an
extended conversation at her home in the Pacific Northwest, she spoke about
her experience of caring for her mother until she died in her nineties. Sylvia
recounted that there were great yet simple moments of interaction with her
mother that were absolutely delightful. At times, she felt that her commit-

ment to care for her mother was part of the good daughter role she sincerely wanted to take on. And as a woman, she sometimes asked herself when she would get to live her own life without the emotional entanglements that developed from her loving but intense relationship with her mother.

Yet it was precisely in the tension of these opposing thoughts and feelings that Sylvia experienced personal growth in caring for her mother over several years. In the act of devotion, she found herself to be supported by new strengths that she did not know she had. Reflecting back on those years, Sylvia feels a great contentment at having given so much of herself to the mutual love that she shared with her mother. In that selfless giving, so much was received.

In his book on aging, changing and dying, *Still Here*, the former Harvard psychologist Richard Alpert, also known as Ram Dass, recounts the opposing inner dynamics he experienced while caring for his father. "At first, I could not help but view Dad's illness as an intrusion on my life, and on all the things I wanted to be doing." Reflecting on his past, Ram Dass remarked in his book that he had felt repeatedly misunderstood by his family and as a result had distanced himself from them. His father had never acknowledged nor understood the value of Ram Dass's intensive spiritual practice and authentic leadership in the greater consciousness movement, particularly during the 1970s and 1980s.

Ram Dass points out that in order to respond mindfully to the needs of others, we must first examine our attachment to the way we believe our life should be, who we are and what we "should" be doing. As he moved through an in-depth examination of his own feelings, Ram Dass noticed that he was sincerely pleased to get into the role of being a dutiful son toward his father. And, as time went on, he moved past this ego-bounded way of accepting his caregiving responsibilities to find that he and his dad were "just two people hanging out together." More than being father and son, they were "souls exchanging love." What's more, Ram Dass writes: "By the time Dad died, I realized that I had been given an incredible gift, and was extremely grateful for having been shaken out of my egocentric attachment to external 'freedom' and the way I thought my life was supposed to be. . . . Caring for Dad, as he cared for me when I was a child, gave me a sense of harmony and completion."

Ram Dass's account reveals the deep personal enrichment one can draw from moving beyond one's role and onto the spiritual path of becoming a soul exchanging love while caregiving. This way of experiencing caregiving is most accessible to those who can draw profound spiritual wisdom from their circumstances, as difficult as this can be at times. For others, being a caregiver in midlife and or retirement may be perceived as filled with burdensome challenges. Of utmost importance, one must cultivate the ability to know when the limits of one's caregiving capacity have been reached. In such times, enlisting the assistance of others is crucial to prevent an inner depletion that can lead to the loss of one's own well-being.

As an unmarried woman in midlife, attending to my professional life as well as my teenage children can, at times, make me feel as though I am submerged by multiple demands. When I feel this way, I sometimes review and change my expectations of my children in order to encourage greater independence and to support them in taking on some new responsibilities. Other times, I may decide that a certain demand from them corresponds to an important need, and I willingly adjust my schedule to accommodate my teenage children. In the end, it always feels worthwhile attending to my teenagers as they make their way to adulthood.

While you move through midlife and into some form of re-engagement, opportunities will emerge along with the potential for new or renewed relationships. Whatever our endeavors may be, universal truths of the power of love, oneness and commitment can be embraced and find expression in all of our relationships. May you joyfully thrive in the grand relational dance with yourself, with others near and far, and within the collectivity to which you belong.

Questions to ponder

- What range of emotions have you experienced around those you have worked with in the past or are currently working with? How have these emotions affected you at work and now, if you have retired?
- If you were to become your own best friend, what would you do to honor and nurture this friendship?
- Identify the kinds of relationships you might like to develop in your retirement or re-engagement years. These could include relationships with

people you mentor, counsel or volunteer with, as well as friendships or partnerships.

- What are the ways, if any, in which you may have unconsciously developed a limiting perception of your significant other?
- How do you see yourself and your role in relation to your family and community in five, ten or twenty years from now?

CHAPTER 8

Wellness from the Inside Out

*The greatest wealth
is health.*

—Virgil

In the past couple of decades, stunning technological advances in medicine have been saving more and more lives and enabling us to live longer, healthier lives. In contrast to these breakthroughs, the definition of health has not much advanced, for good health is still often defined as the absence of disease. As you may have observed, many Western medical practitioners continue to view the body as a mechanistic assemblage of parts rather than an organic whole. Some scientists and physicians still have difficulty understanding what really creates well-being and health. Looking at the word "disease" itself, we find that the key to real health is right there, as a discreet yet obvious clue. Dis-ease is a state in which the ease, flow and harmony of true health has been disturbed. In this chapter, you will read about new areas of medicine, as well as practices conducive to wellness. I also share an inspiring story of healing in midlife.

Energy and mind over health

Recently, I have been fascinated by the proliferation of pioneers of alternative practices who are increasingly being heard as they cause ripples in the fields of wellness and medicine. The pioneers include physicians who have been urging us to look at the power of love and of our mind to affect our health. The well-known physician Patch Adams speaks frequently about the importance of love in healing. Dr. Bernie Siegel, author of *Love, Medicine and Miracles*, has also been outspoken about what is really conducive to well-being and vitality. Dr. Larry Dosey, author of several books including *The Extraordinary Healing Power of Ordinary Things*, has conducted scientific studies on the amazing power of prayer to help people heal. These names are just a few among the many helping us to become more aware of the invisible forces that are either conducive to health or that disrupt the flow and lead to dis-ease.

In the field of energy medicine, new discoveries are rapidly shedding light on some of those invisible forces in health and healing. In *Soul Medicine: Awakening Your Inner Blueprint for Abundant Health and Energy*, the authors Dr. Norman Shealy and Dawson Church discuss the implications of research from the discipline of epigenetics, the study of heritable changes in gene function that occur without a change in the DNA sequence. The old view that our genes determine our physical characteristics, disease propensity and some behaviors is being replaced by a new view. Church and Shealy write, according to the scientist Karl Maret, MD, "Genomes are plastic and resemble constantly rewritten software code rather than being fixed hardware that you inherit at birth." What then influences how genomes are being "rewritten" is part of the subject of Dawson Church's new book, *The Genie in Your Genes: Epigenetic Medicine and the New Biology of Intention*, which explains the interconnections between our thoughts, our beliefs, our intentions, and our genes and cells.

In a seminar presented by Dr. Bruce Lipton, cellular biologist and author of *The Biology of Belief*, I was captivated while hearing about how our will to survive transpires at the cellular level. Lipton explained that as humans, we hold within our multicellular organism the biological imperative that is the impulse and desire to maintain our existence. Reflecting this survival instinct, our cells are programmed for growth and/or protection modes of behavior. Similarly, but on the macro psychosocial/behavioral level, in response to our perception of a given stimulus in our environment, we tend to be either attracted or repelled. If we perceive the stimulus to be appealing—life-enhancing—we respond by going with the flow of attraction or love, thereby supporting our growth and vitality at the cellular level. Conversely, if we often perceive people or things in our environment as dangerous—life-threatening—we end up in protection mode, which consumes energy and prevents the continuous growth necessary to maintain the flow of life within.

Unfortunately, over the years, unfinished business, unaddressed trauma and fears of all kinds tend to accumulate in our subconscious mind and may lead us into a state of chronic tension and protection. Sometimes, the illnesses or deaths of those around us can also influence us to become fearful of life's unpredictability and of the process of aging. You likely know of people who seemed to have done everything they could to be in full health and yet suddenly became seriously ill and died relatively quickly. When this happens around you, you may become fearful that the same could happen to you. Experiencing sudden losses of loved ones reminds us of the precariousness of our life and that there is no guarantee that our healthy lifestyle will promote longevity.

In the area of health, as in all other aspects of life, we cannot underestimate the power of our mind to contribute to our well-being. Evidently, cultivating inner peace and living authentically with a sense of engagement are most conducive to the vitality that is at the heart of true well-being. Health is optimized when we take responsibility for ourselves, embrace rather than store up our emotions, and nurture thoughts in harmony with wellness. As our positive thoughts and emotions guide our intentions and actions, we can continue to develop lifestyle habits and practices that are commensurate with the state of health we desire.

The current state of health among us

Across the diversity among boomers, there are great differences in the ways in which people take responsibility for their health and wellness. At the start of 2006 in Canada, the Canadian Heart and Stroke Foundation issued a health report based on their research. Statistics revealed that 1.3 million people, or 21 percent of boomers between the ages of 45 and 49, had already been diagnosed with heart disease, stroke or high blood pressure. The study also revealed that more than 40 percent of Canadians in their sixties had cardiovascular disease.

Based on data collected through the Canadian Community Health Survey in 2003–04, the report found that 52 percent of boomers were leading a sedentary lifestyle in 2006, compared to 43 percent ten years previously. Factors contributing to this decline in activity included the long commute made by many suburbanites on a daily basis. As many of us spend hours each day on the road *to and from* work, and also sit most of the day *at* work, our bodies are deprived of physical activity. When it comes to generating and using energy, the old saying "Use it or lose it" seems to be true. Fortunately, according to my informal research, many of those who opt for a partial retirement are eager to develop a regimen that includes various forms of physical activities to achieve better life balance. Having started to attend Hatha yoga classes regularly at age 51, I am grateful that this body-mind-spirit practice has generated more flexibility in my body and more calmness in my nervous system and state of being. Along with other forms of movements such as dancing, cycling and walking, I expect to continue *using* my energy to keep it flowing well into my sunset years.

Issues of self-esteem, especially those linked to body image, are also potential factors leading to poor health. Although the majority of people know what is conducive to well-being, those who have an impoverished self-concept are more likely to develop self-sabotaging patterns that undermine their wellness. These patterns include emotional overeating, waiting for external circumstances to motivate ourselves to exercise, insufficient sleep from keeping overly busy, alcohol abuse to numb out unresolved inner conflicts, and so on. Paradoxically, the shift of one's orientation toward full health includes unconditional acceptance for ourself and our physical body *as it is.* While we learn to honor and embrace the sacredness of the life energy within, we better enable that force to lead and restore us to our natural state, which is vibrant health. Additionally, through the worthwhile actions we can take daily to nourish ourselves and sustain our vitality, we are capable of enhancing the flow of our life toward growth and love rather than fear and protection.

Rich's miraculous story of midlife healing

Those of us who suddenly come face to face with a serious illness are given an unprecedented opportunity to grow in love and gratitude while we heal. This was the experience of Rich Henry, co-founder of For the GrandChildren, whom I met in Seattle, near the end of his healing journey.

After noticing some slight confusion in his mind and subtle changes in his perception while attending a conference in Chicago in July 2006, Rich got medical attention and underwent an MRI procedure. On the day he and his wife Ruth Ann were in the doctor's office for the results, three shocking sentences stood out from what the doctor said: "I have hard news. You have a brain tumor. Put your affairs in order." Rich was scheduled for immediate brain surgery to remove the tumor. He became very clear about the importance of responding to the cancer with mindfulness. "I can't choose not to have the tumor," he told himself, "but I can choose how I will respond." Supported by his loved ones, Rich drew upon new depths of courage and passed through a series of profound learning episodes while overcoming this period of adversity.

As much as this illness was an intensely personal experience, Rich knew that the cancer was also a metaphor for the collective form of dis-ease that all of us have inadvertently contributed to creating on this planet. This metaphor is conveyed in a deep ecology quote by Brian Patrick in Brad Blanton's book *Practicing Radical Honesty: How to Complete the Past, Live in the Present and Build a Future*.

> A cancer cell is a normal cell disconnected from its genetic memory, cut off from the wisdom of millions of years of evolutionary development. It doesn't cooperate in harmony with the rest of the body. It experiences itself as separate from the body, overpopulates, and consumes the organism which supports it. Cancer eventually kills itself by consuming its own environment.

While on one level Rich saw himself as a microcosm in the cosmos we all share, at the same time he felt that it was best for him not to identify with the cancer as being "his."

On the morning following the brain surgery, he gradually awoke within blissful, expanded qualities of consciousness. In this state, Rich had transcended the illusion of separateness and experienced himself as being one with all creation. This was a boundless and timeless space in which he felt at one with the universe. Although he had long believed in and sought this transcended way of being as part of his spiritual quest, once in the midst of it, Rich was awestruck as "all the words fell away." During his recovery, Rich walked his healing path with outstanding teams of medical professionals he found at the University of Washington and Duke University plus other complementary medicine practitioners.

When he was first diagnosed, Rich was shown daunting statistics for his condition and told, "You'll be really lucky to make it a year." But Rich knew that his life was not to be minimized or defined by these numbers. Aided by his loving family and supportive doctors, Rich stayed mindfully and lovingly focused on his recovery and on rebuilding his health. Through various practices conducive to wellness, such as meditation and visualization, Rich was a clear channel, open to the divine process of healing. Eighteen months after he was diagnosed, the MRI and PET scans of his brain revealed no traces of cancer. Rich considers his "adventure," as he refers to it, a great blessing and teaching. He is now more vibrantly alive than ever before as he continues on his journey of purposeful contribution.

Meditating into well-being

In the midst of our increasingly hectic lives, many of us have been drawn to the practice of meditation as an oasis from which to appease our thirst for quiet moments. Aside from meditation helping us to become more mindful of our thoughts, we can also use it to *change our relationship* to our thoughts. Over time, we are able to see that thoughts pass through our minds as clouds move across the vastness of the sky. We realize, as I mentioned in chapter 6 about freedom, that we don't have to believe or identify with our thoughts. By loosening the hold our mind has on the content of our thinking, we can more easily place our attention on thoughts that support us and enhance our wellness.

Although most people are aware that meditation also alleviates stress, studies now show that it can actually cause positive changes in the brain. The January 2006 issue of *Time* magazine reported findings of a study on meditation conducted by the research scientist Sara Lazar. This study showed that the gray matter in the brains of twenty men and women from the Boston area who meditated forty minutes a day was thicker than that of people who did not meditate. Lazar states that, in contrast to previous studies involving Buddhist monks, her study showed, for the first time, that you do not need to meditate all day to achieve similar optimizing of brain functions that results from more gray matter.

What is more, Lazar's research suggests that meditation may slow the natural thinning of a section of the cortex that occurs in varying degrees with advancement of age. This finding is further supported by about six hundred controlled studies reported to have taken place since the mid-seventies on the benefits of meditation and particularly the use of Transcendental Meditation. As distinct from mindfulness meditation, which focuses on the breath, Transcendental Meditation uses a mantra as a tool on which to focus one's mind. In *Meditation as Medicine*, the authors Dharma Singh Khalsa, MD, and Cameron Stauth report that out of those six hundred studies on the use of the Transcendental Meditation program, proven achievable benefits include the following:

- reduction of anxiety
- reduction of chronic pain
- lowered levels of cortisol
- increase in cognitive function
- reduction of substance abuse
- lowered blood pressure
- improvement in post-traumatic stress syndrome
- reduction in use of medical care and hospitalization

Meditation was surely an important part of Rich's recovery. Even when we are enjoying good health, the multiple benefits of this practice speak to the importance of integrating or sustaining it throughout our life to reap its worthwhile rewards.

Tapping the intelligence of the heart

An emphatic *yes!* is what I heard within me when I first discovered Heart-Math. This research and education organization has developed innovative tools and technologies at the crossroads of psychology and physiology. Its work and philosophy affirmed my own intuitive validation of the heart's way of knowing. Indeed, across all cultures we can find themes of acknowledgment of the heart's wisdom. But as you may have experienced, although our Western culture may encourage us to "follow our heart," in reality, few people allow themselves to live in full congruence with the wisdom of their heart. The HeartMath website (listed in the resources section) provides detailed information about the group's research, programs and tools designed to help people tap into and integrate this kind of intelligence in their life.

HeartMath has proven that the heart is far more than a muscle to pump blood. It is also a sensory organ and a sophisticated information processing center. Moreover, the heart has been found to have its own nervous system, which gives it the ability to sense, learn, remember and make functional decisions independent of the brain. In its interconnectedness with the rest of the body, the heart sends powerful signals in four different ways: neurologically, bio-physically, hormonally and energetically.

If you are at the threshold of retirement, you may have, knowingly or not, accumulated frustration and irritation at work that has disrupted the flow of energy within you. HeartMath's researchers have discovered that the heart's beat-to-beat rhythmic pattern, called heart rate variability or HRV, is very sensitive to emotional states. In *Transforming Anger*, by Doc Childre (founder of HeartMath) and Deborah Rozman, the authors explain that when you experience stressful emotions such as anger and frustration, your HRV pattern has a disordered and chaotic rhythm. This is referred to as *incoherent HRV pattern*, in which the heart's rhythm is characterized by irregularity.

Displayed on a graph, the rhythm pattern of a frustrated and angry person's heart would look rough and jagged, much like the kinds of emotions that tend to inhabit this person. This correlation between emotions and heart rhythms was also confirmed by Deepak Chopra, MD, who has stated that negative emotions such as anger held within tend to lead to arrhythmia, a condition in which the heart beats in irregular rhythms. In my own research for this book, I learned from a police officer that when people retire from such high-stress, emotionally intense work, they are at high risk of having a heart attack.

In contrast to the effect of high stress and negative emotions on the heart, maintaining positive emotions greatly contributes to our well-being.

Compared to the irregular rhythm precipitated by stress, the heart rhythm of a person experiencing appreciation or other positive emotions displays coherence. On a graph, this pattern has a smooth regularity that reflects the state of calm and poise associated with positive emotions. Besides the work of Childre and Chopra, much other research and many more books now show the undeniable connection between loving inner states and vibrant health.

In the spirit of truth and acceptance

In keeping with this book's emphasis on the importance of being true to oneself, here is yet another study showing the connection between inner congruence and health. In the *Ode* magazine of December 2007, David Servan-Schreiber, MD, author of *Healing Without Freud or Prozac*, reports findings from Professor Steve Cole at the University of California in Los Angeles. Cole and his colleagues studied more than two hundred homosexual men over five years and concluded that "those who chose to conceal their homosexuality were three times more likely to develop cancer or a serious infection." This, affirms Servan-Schreiber, shows that for our immune system to function most effectively, we need to live authentically, in truth and harmony with ourselves. Such a study reinforces the assertions of Dr. Lipton (*The Biology of Belief*) about the health benefits of maintaining an attitude of openness rather than one in which we often recoil in protection mode.

Despite our best efforts to sustain health-promoting habits and being true to ourselves, some factors affecting our wellness are beyond our control. These include the toxins in our environment, the cumulative effects of chemicals in food and a variety of other factors we do not even know. With the process of aging, some of our physical and mental abilities may eventually be diminished, but let us not *expect* this to happen before it occurs. Numerous examples of people thriving in their nineties encourage us to expect to remain vitally alive well into advanced eldership.

One of my friends, Jan Furst, turned 95 in January 2008. During his nineties, he still enjoyed fencing as one of his activities and he completed and published his third book. During a conversation over a delicious dinner he had prepared at his house, I asked him about his health. He said: "I have arthritis in one knee but otherwise I'm just fine." He once told me that he wakes up singing daily because he is so happy to be alive. Jan is a model of gracious, joyful and successful aging. He is the person I think of when I tell others that "aging is inevitable but getting old is optional."

In spite of the possible decline in energy we may eventually encounter, we will tend to develop wisdom along with an astute ability to economize and maximize the use of our energy. In his book *Crossing the Unknown Sea*, David Whyte writes about a very old but highly skilled sheep dog that lived in Ireland years ago. Whyte explains that while the younger dogs would make great sweeping motions to get the sheep to move, this old dog no longer had to expend that much energy to get the same result. He would take a few steps at the exact and precise place on the hill that would motivate the sheep to move where they were required to go. Unless we develop an illness that affects our brain and its faculties, this kind of economy of means becomes more and more available to us as we age. If we can remain acutely aware of our experiences and our surrounding environment as we keep shaping the course of our life, we are better able to adjust to changing circumstances.

In the next chapter, you will read inspiring stories and information to sharpen your awareness of the lifestyle choices, including travel choices, you are about to make during the next precious decades of your life.

Questions to ponder

- What beliefs do you hold about your ability to nurture or further improve your health?
- What, if any, self-sabotaging patterns do you want to let go of to generate more well-being in yourself?
- What are some of the health-enhancing habits and practices you would like to develop to augment your wellness?
- How could you modify your daily life in order to incorporate these health-promoting activities and choices?
- In various areas of your life, what positive expectations and/or fears do you have about advanced eldership?

CHAPTER 9

Lifestyle Choices
That Fulfill

*I am not interested so much in what I do with my
hands or words as what I do with my heart. I want to
live from the inside out, not from the outside in.*

—Hugh Prather

Does your lifestyle reflect an intention to live "from the inside out"?
When we embrace this way of living, intent on following our heart,
we are inwardly guided to make choices more conducive to our well-being
and to our fulfillment. Those who have succeeded at earning their livelihood
from their talents and their passions do not generally have an intense need
for a lot of leisure, entertainment or rest to reward themselves. If or when
they retire, such people are more likely to seek a balanced life conducive to
their continuing growth, to meaningful contribution and to the pure enjoyment of life's precious moments. Here you will read about lifestyle
choices that include contemplation, pleasure, travel and social utility, life
lived at a pace that enables one to enjoy *quality* more than *quantity* in life.

Reassessing your habits

After I spoke at a gathering of lawyers about the new paradigm of "retirement" a couple of years ago, I heard one of them say: "You're right, Isabelle, golfing is not going to be enough to keep me happy after I retire next year." I sensed this man's anxiety as he talked about figuring out how he would find meaning and what lifestyle choices he was going to make for the years ahead. Long ago, he had probably adopted the belief that retirement was primarily about rest, relaxation and pleasure-seeking, but now he knew that this would not lead him to happiness.

In the process of re-engagement, you may become aware that some of your current practices and habits contribute to your well-being, while other habits have become obsolete and no longer serve you. Naturally, we tend to hold onto old habits just because we have settled into their tracks. But to the degree that we want to keep growing and feel alive, we must reassess our habits from time to time and avoid letting them constrict us.

Ideally, we all strive for a balance of change and stability. If your habits are not mindfully chosen according to what is most important to you, you may later have regrets and feel that life has passed you by. Granted, as relational beings we are impacted by those around us and some of our activities and habits are adopted in response to the needs of those around us. Yet, at any time, you can proactively instigate change and adopt new attitudes and habits that will support your intention to shape your life into a masterpiece. As Socrates hinted when he said that "the unexamined life is not worth living," unexamined routines can keep us in an automatic mode of living that gradually leads toward disengagement from the life force within and the world around us. Examining your life can simply mean that you make room for contemplation, for reflection and perhaps for forms of creative expression that foster your ability to "know thyself," as Socrates suggested.

The gift of contemplation and creativity

Contemplative practices such as meditation and reflecting on or delighting in nature enable us to live in greater harmony with the invisible dimensions of life, the true sources of fulfillment. As well, these practices bring richness to our lives because they require us to be fully present. When I visit my friend Larry Robinson in Sebastopol, California—whose story is told in chapter

5—I am struck by his ability to contemplate the beauty of nature around him. Every day he looks out at the many birds that inhabit or visit the trees on his property. In an instant of contemplation, Larry delights in the experience of the beauty he observes. This practice nourishes his soul and enhances the quality of his life. Even in space-limited urban settings, everyone can find ways to create a contemplative space in their immediate environment, at a nearby park or in a waterfront area.

Larry also sends a poem every day to his friends and e-mail community. Poetry is a lovely way to add a moment of contemplation in your day. It helps you to maintain a relationship with the mysterious, to be reminded of the intangible things that matter, and to pause for a moment in the midst of the current fast pace of our culture. Through poetry and by marveling over nature's beauty on a regular basis, we tend to slow down and cultivate a mindset of gratitude, which is conducive to experiencing contentment.

Contemplation can also become a wondrous gateway into self-expression. When we are inspired by what we see, feel, hear or read, we are more naturally inclined toward dwelling in our own creativity. Making space in your lifestyle for creative endeavors can counteract the risk of settling into an overly predictable routine in which your habits become devoid of real joy or spontaneity.

Midlife and re-engagement often stimulate the re-awakening of the creative impulse that may have been dormant within. Whether expressed through music, arts, singing, crafts or any other passion, creative expression always has a restorative effect on the soul. And the loosening of inhibitions that often occurs in one's second life is like the wind in our sails infusing energy into our creative quests. Even those who think they are not inclined this way may, to their surprise, delight in new and varied forms of self-expression while approaching eldership. I recall observing pride and joy on my father's face when he showed me the stained-glass lamp he had completed during a course he attended following his retirement.

The call of nature and simplicity

At the start of this writing project, I stayed at a friend's house on a nearby nature-filled island while she was away on vacation. When I returned and drove through downtown Vancouver, a strong physical sensation came up within me. I felt oppressed by the massive structures of concrete and glass towering over the streets, reducing the spaciousness of the sky. Suddenly, I realized that I was no longer being held in the arms of Mother Nature as the urban sprawl surrounded me. Through this experience, I realized to what extent nature had been soothing my soul over the previous couple of weeks. And that the pace of life on the island was so much more conducive to the rhythms of graceful living I had been yearning for.

Perhaps you have also felt the longing to live closer to the natural world, if you are not already there. A number of people I know spend part of each year in natural settings, the rest in urban areas. If this appeals, you may gradually make changes enabling you to combine your interests, your activities and the places you most desire to live. Looking at your life with the intent to simplify it, especially if you are entering retirement, will help you create the conditions most conducive to alternating between two places of residence. Choosing to live in natural surroundings facilitates the process of simplification because Nature is a great model of sufficiency unto itself. And being in the richness of nature leads us more easily to a sense of contentment. As you attune yourself to the seasons, which are more visible in natural environments, you tend to be more attentive to your own inner seasons and rhythms.

Dr. John Zelenski, a psychologist at Carleton University in Ottawa, has been involved in research to learn more about the human condition of happiness. As reported by Joanne Laucius in the *Vancouver Sun*, Zelenski's research led him to look at the symbiotic relationship between nature and human happiness. He and his team developed a questionnaire on "nature-relatedness" that was then answered by hundreds of people, primarily executives and students. Results revealed that "people who felt connected to nature also had a sense of purpose in life and more self-acceptance," both of which contribute greatly to happiness. Through his research Zelenski validates what most of us intuitively know, that people who are close to nature are happier and they tend to live eco-friendly lives in voluntary simplicity.

Live simply so that others may simply live.
—MOHANDAS GANDHI

In Western culture, simplicity is still sometimes mistaken for a virtuous lifestyle in which we sacrifice the luxuries and comforts we may feel we have earned through hard work or from our social status. In the anthology *Ecopsychology*, Allen Kanner and Mary Gomes point out that it is the false consumer self in us that tends to resist a more simple way of life. These authors also note that the false self or consumer self is an identity many of us have unconsciously taken on. It is false because it arises from "a merciless distortion of authentic human needs and desires." That distortion is a significant factor in the widespread dissatisfaction and unhappiness in Western culture. While our minds have been influenced to seek more and more material goods and comforts, the needs of our souls have been increasingly disregarded and devalued. Generally, the more we have, the less we tend to appreciate and the less we are satisfied.

Simplifying can merely mean that you selectively choose to surround yourself with things that serve your "authentic human needs." These are the things that most nurture your aliveness. Choosing simplicity, you would consume what you need and enjoy, and release any excess of material possessions that would otherwise constrict the flow of energy and renewal. You would also avoid accumulating clutter, which can foster stagnation. By living simply, you better embrace your share of the collective responsibility we all have to refrain from overconsuming.

Typically, the passage of time advances most of us toward simplicity and the values that favor the intangible dimensions of life. While we move forward in our psycho-spiritual development, we are drawn into a deeper appreciation for the richness in simple moments. Increasingly, we want to shape our life so that it becomes more satisfying on the *qualitative* level rather than on the *quantitative* level. We tend to shift our sense of worth away from material things, toward that which is invisible but holds greater meaning. It is important that you recognize this shift in you because it gives you a new frame of reference, like a bridge into a new orientation, from which you can make more fulfilling lifestyle choices.

With this increasing detachment from material things, we also gain a deeper appreciation of the presence of others in our lives. Like many of the people featured in this book, you may notice that giving of yourself or helping others provides inner nourishment unequalled by any material rewards.

And sometimes, as it did for Janey Talbot (see chapter 4), the desire to be of service arises in the midst of our travels and exposure to other cultures.

Traveling for exploration, contribution and fulfillment

Travel is fatal to prejudice, bigotry and narrow mindedness.
Broad, wholesome, charitable views cannot be acquired by
vegetating in one little corner of the earth.
— MARK TWAIN

In light of the increasing concerns over global warming and everything that contributes to it, traveling has become a somewhat controversial activity. But when your travel is something you "do with your heart," as in the quote from Hugh Prather at the beginning of this chapter, when it benefits others as well as yourself, then it is worthwhile. While we connect with others in developing countries, like several people whose stories are included in this book, we can begin to see ourselves as global citizens. Then we feel motivated to help diminish the gap between those who are rich with opportunities and material resources and those who are not.

Many new options have recently arisen for travel to become a pilgrimage, an odyssey of self-discovery or an altruistic journey. From sacred sites tours to vision quests, including ecotourism, numerous options now abound, and several possibilities are listed in the resources section of this book. As part of this trend, new distinctions are being made between sustainable tourism and geotourism. The latter means that in addition to minimizing one's footprint as a tourist, you also celebrate the environment you visit. As advised by Jonathan Tourtellot, editor of *National Geographic Traveler*, "Think of every bill in your pocket as a vote. When you spend it, you are voting for what you want to see more of in this place."

Among the many organizations that offer ways to be fulfilled and contribute, Builders Without Borders is a wonderful example (see chapter 6). For those who like to develop or build something of a tangible nature, this organization leads people in the rewarding activities of creating buildings of great use to communities in foreign countries. Some travel companies now include various forms of altruism in action or sacred sites visits among the opportunities they offer. I still recall vividly the description of the Great

Wall of China shared by my friend Nancy Klinkhamer, founder of Turn Your Face to the Sun Travel (website listed in resources section). Thinking back to her unforgettable visit, she said:

> I can still see myself standing on the Great Wall deeply impacted by what I felt and saw there. We got to go further than most tourists do, and I realized the implication of being on the wall, where many people had lost their lives in the process of building it. And because those people were buried in the wall, I was suddenly awestruck with the feeling that I was actually standing on a great monument. As I looked out, the mist was starting to rise and it covered the wall except for the towers and it went on as far as I could see. What really hit me then was that we often struggle through our lives, easily forgetting that even the small actions we take can have significant impact on people. I thought about the cumulative effect of all the actions taken by each person, to create something of this magnitude, and I felt a mixture of humility and greatness at the same time.

While she recounted this incredible experience, Nancy added that it was there on the Great Wall that she fully realized, on a deep gut level, that everything we do has a ripple effect.

In the book *Claiming Your Place at the Fire*, co-author Richard J. Leider talks about his journeys leading groups of "inventurers," people who adventure inward through outdoor experiences. For many years, Leider has been taking groups of men to the part of Africa that is inhabited by the Hadza, tribes of hunter-gatherers. Interviewed on an Internet radio station, Leider affirmed that these expeditions are not just trips but they are more like an odyssey. Men do not go there to "solve problems," he said, but to take "a deep dive into themselves." In these "inventures" participants finally have the chance, with the support of others, to contemplate the deep questions of their life in a completely different environment.

In this natural yet unfamiliar social context, the men cannot operate in automatic mode; they are forced into deeper levels of presence, attention and conversation. This type of journey allows participants to enter fully in the developmental transition that has often called their attention for years. Far away from the distractions and habits of modern, fast-paced life, these men are better able to experience profound, life-changing truths drawn to the surface from the underground channels of transition. In a condensed and intensified "inventure," these men can move through the stages of letting go of what has hindered them, traverse the zone of fears and doubts, and finally envision a creative new beginning. Among the many choices you will make in midlife or in your re-engagement, journeys such as these keep you oriented toward fulfillment because of the deep revelations they allow you to access.

Marcia Jaffe, a resident of Sausalito, California, had a profound life-changing experience when she traveled to Bali on her own for the first time in 2003.

Marcia's extraordinary story

Marcia Jaffe took a short holiday to Bali, Indonesia, in October 2003 to recuperate from producing a 2,000-person conference in California. She was certain that there were no more conferences in her future, for she was tired and ready for something new. Without quite knowing why, Bali was not just a destination she was drawn to, it felt like a "calling." While traveling in Ubud, a cultural center on the island, she found herself in dialogue with numerous Balinese and was drawn to their spiritual way of being and their community life. But it was the Balinese reaction to the terrorist's bomb that exploded in Denpasar, Bali, in 2002 that was most astounding to her. Rather than retaliate, the Balinese inquired within themselves, wondering what they might have done that contributed to causing this tragedy while pondering what they could do to prevent this from occurring again.

During her time in Bali, one year after the explosion, Marcia observed that the Balinese were economically strained and in desperate need to have tourists come back, because Bali's economic structure is largely based on tourism. Feeling moved to help and support the people of this beautiful island, Marcia began to envision a way to bring people together to learn from the Balinese's way of embodying peace and honoring the sacred. Upon her return home to Sausalito, California, Marcia teamed up with two other deeply committed and well-seasoned professionals, Wilford Welch and Carole Angermier. As result, the first Quest for Global Healing conference was held in December 2004, attended by more than 425 people from 22 countries. In the chapter "Women Ushering in the Future," you can read more about what Marcia and her team created following this hugely successful event.

Offering joy and compassion across the miles

> *Too often we underestimate the power of touch,*
> *a smile, a kind word, a listening ear, an honest compliment,*
> *or the smallest act of caring, all of which have*
> *the potential to turn a life around.*
> — LEO BUSCAGLIA

When I first heard about the Quest for Global Healing from Lynne Twist in September 2004, I was irresistibly drawn to attend. Since the first time I traveled to Bali, Indonesia, for that conference in December 2004, my life has changed in several wonderful ways. You will read more about this in chapter 14.

My own desire to travel in a way that combines exploration and service was further stimulated by meeting Patch Adams in 2006. After hearing about the clowning tours he had been leading, I became attracted to this kind of experience. Then I found out from Patch that tours were also being led by his friends and colleagues in Italy. In July 2006, I joined a group of twenty people from seven countries with Italo and Genevra as our leaders across Sicily. These long-term colleagues of Patch Adams share the same contagious spirit of passionate devotion to clowning as a way of bridging the gaps that separate so many of us in this world.

Over the ten days of the tour, I experienced many heart-warming moments and magical instances of connecting with others through the simplicity of a smile, touch, warm eye contact, music or humor. For the tour I wore colorful clothing; a golden heart adorned my head, and a large velvety smiling flower encircled my neck. As our group arrived in a hospital, with all of our bright colors and musical sounds, we would dispel the atmosphere that had sometimes become too solemn or serious. In fact, on the trip I gained a new understanding of the expression "dead serious"—some of the doctors we encountered were so deadly serious that their intervention would not likely be conducive to healing, I thought. But other doctors joined us, eager to partake in our contagious lightness of being as we spread joy through their institution.

In one particularly memorable moment, several doctors and nurses joined us and our music in a spontaneous dance in the middle of a hallway. The only difficulty, for me, was trying to hold back my welling tears of joy. As the medical staff danced with us, they rejoined their own creative, childlike precious selves. They were suddenly freed from the bounds of their professional roles, affirming the value of joy and of embracing our shared moments passionately.

On the palliative care ward in one hospital, a woman standing by her husband's bed invited the small group we had formed on that floor to enter her husband's room. Despite his advanced age and illness, this man suddenly became radiant as he talked with us and we listened. Then he asked a few women in our group to give him a kiss, saying that he always wanted to get a kiss from beautiful women, in addition to the kisses he got from his wife. His eyes glittered with enjoyment as we kissed him. During our tour, it was evident that we helped people to let go of their inhibitions while they were in the grip of their health challenges or even at death's doorway. With our joy and warmth, we reminded them that life was worth living, all the way to the last moments.

When our group visited hospitals for children, I noticed that some of the young patients were a little frightened of us at first because we looked and sounded quite boisterous and bold. But then, as we approached them gently, sometimes even tenderly, or with humor and joy, they started to smile as they became engaged in the interaction. I have a particularly fond memory of observing the transformation in a teenage girl with Down syndrome. At an event for teens with special needs, a girl named Lisa was quite reluctant to join us at first. But after observing us dance to the music we were playing, she came into our midst and started to dance with a big smile on her face. At one point I looked at her and thought, *Ahhhh, she has now freed herself into exuberance.* It was beautiful and moving to witness that transformation.

A few weeks after this journey, an e-mail from our leader Genevra reported that she had had many positive comments from the staff in the hospitals. Better still, Genevra informed the group that some of the doctors said we had created a positive change in the atmosphere of the hospital. This gave me a deep sense of satisfaction. It was an affirmation of the lasting impact of what we can do when we do it sincerely, in the spirit of service, in a microcosm of humanity.

In the next chapter, you are invited to reflect on your relationship with time and how you apportion your energy. When you refrain from packing your days with time-filling activities, you are better able to make choices conducive to the fulfilling lifestyle you desire.

Questions to ponder

- How does the desire to "follow your heart" manifest in your lifestyle choices?
- Looking into your daily habits, which ones, if any, no longer contribute to your happiness? What habits would you like to change?
- What talent or passion in you is seeking to be expressed creatively at this time in your life?
- How has your increased appreciation for quality versus quantity manifested in your life?
- Which of your values generally guides your travel choices?
- What part of the world and culture are you most drawn to at this time, and why?

CHAPTER 10

Balancing Time and Energy

To get all there is out of living, we must employ
our time wisely, never being in too much of a hurry
to stop and sip life, but never losing our sense
of the enormous value of a minute.

— Robert Updegraff

If Time had a voice, I once imagined that it would have a pertinent message to communicate to those of us who struggle against it. Here is an excerpt from my poem "From the Voice of Time":

Many of you attempt to save me or manage me.

But despite your efforts, I remain unchanged.

Yet I bring forth change itself as surely as the sun rises over the horizon at dawn.

When you are in a frantic race against me, you fail to hear the gentle whispers of your soul.

In spite of your insistence on declaring me insufficient, I persist in giving you the chance to savour the moments afforded by the breath of your life.

And as you do so, you will find plenty of now-ness in each and every instant.

When I first went to Ubud in Bali, Indonesia, for the Quest for Global Healing conference in 2004, I was struck by the realization that this was a place where one could just "be." Here, it seemed to me, I could stop feeling caught in the ever-present race against time that many of us experience in the West. Within twenty-four hours after landing in Bali, I found myself slipping, as smoothly as silk, into a rhythm that felt much more soul-friendly than the Western pace of life. As I experienced more of the culture in Bali, I felt the sense of significance, sacredness and gratitude that is woven into the Balinese way of life and community.

In contrast to this, I recall going through years of pushing all day against the tight grip of time in my work as a social worker, nearly a decade ago. For years, you may also have experienced this time pressure as a suffocating force upon your throat. Perhaps you have been awakened by the clock, that petty tyrant insisting you arise no matter how tired you are. How you look forward to having more time in retirement! Ironically, you cannot wait to slow down, nudged by an urgency to learn how to savor the moment. Like many others in our society, you may feel that life is speeding ahead while you are breathlessly running behind trying to catch up.

The hunger we collectively share to live each moment fully is evidenced by the success of books such as *The Power of Now* by Eckhart Tolle. Several years ago, this international best seller responded to our yearning to be more at ease with ourselves, more mindful and present. More than this, in *The Power of Now*, and in his most recent book, *A New Earth*, Tolle invites us to change our relationship to time, evolve beyond ego-driven pursuits and infuse a sense of sacredness in what we do. Most people perceive time as a linear span from the past to the future, but this perception varies across cultures. In truth, as Tolle explains, only *this moment* is real and directly available to our experience. The past and the future are either in our memories or in our imagination; either way, they are represented in our minds but do not exist in our immediate sensory experience. Yet, many of us manage to avoid the present as we are caught in our mind's dialogue. Some experience this as a constant chatter aimed at going over past events or at fretting about something in the future. Learning to meet this inner chatter with a compassionate detachment enables you to observe it rather than getting caught in it. Through the cultivation of a quieter mind you can better hear (as in the poem above) "the gentle whispers of your soul," which lead you to live in a way that is attuned to your heart's yearnings.

The hurried pace

Since the start of the Industrial Revolution, Western culture has come to worship speed, to the point of caricature. Of course, technology colludes with us to keep accelerating the fast pace until . . . until . . . we spin ourselves out of our planetary orbit! In the twinkle of an eye, I can picture that—perhaps you can too.

The author Carl Honoré helps readers to challenge the entrapments of our "cult of speed." The following quotation shows how surprisingly early in the past century our ancestors started their love affair with speed: "We affirm that the world's magnificence has been enriched by a new beauty: the beauty of speed." These words are from the Futurist Manifesto of 1909, as quoted in Honoré's book *In Praise of Slowness*

Undoubtedly, the seductively hurried pace of modern life can rob us, if we let it, of the ability to savor our lives. And when we are caught in the frenzy, our days come to resemble the readily replaceable, often disposable objects that surround us. The harmful effects of the "cult of speed" are captured eloquently by Thomas Merton, quoted by Charlie Badenhop in the March 15, 2007 Seishindo newsletter *Pure Heart, Simple Mind*:

> To allow oneself to be carried away by a multitude of conflicting concerns, to surrender to too many demands, to commit to too many projects, to want to help everyone in everything is itself to succumb to the violence of our times. Frenzy destroys our inner capacity for peace. It destroys the fruitfulness of our work, because it kills the root of inner wisdom which makes work fruitful.

Deep down, most of us long to focus on worthwhile activities that have a timeless dimension and larger realms of significance. For some of us, the busyness of our days may be due to ever new technologies that prompt us to do more and do it faster. In an article entitled "How to Put Time on Your Side," published in *Ode* magazine in May 2007, Jon Kabat-Zinn, a renowned meditation teacher, points out that all of our technology-driven habits are taking a toll on our nervous systems. As we are constantly "yanked into the outer world" through technology, we would be wise to "develop a robust counterbalance in the inner world," he suggests, referring to mindfulness practices.

Kabat-Zinn warns us that the pace of our lives is now being partially driven by an exponential acceleration called Moore's Law. The co-founder of Intel, Gordon Moore, first stated this law, which governs the size and speed of integrated circuits. According to Moore's Law, writes Kabat-Zinn, "Every 18 months, the computing power and speed of the next generation of microprocessors doubles while their sizes are cut in half and their cost remains about the same." By the time you read this book, computers are likely to have become yet even smaller and more powerful.

If you are about to enter retirement and attempt to close the door on the winds of frenzy, you will probably realize, at least initially, that slowing down is not as easy as you previously thought. Most of us have been accustomed to filling our days with activities, lined up one after the other. The hurried pace may be comfortable simply because that is what we are habituated to. Our challenge in the process of re-engaging is to recompose our days according to a different cadence, a more organic rhythm that respects the needs of our body as it changes with time. We want to be attuned to an inner rhythm arising out of our core and expressing itself into action without compulsivity and without being overly stressed or rushed.

Think for a moment about music, which is made up of time intervals, notes and rhythms. If the composer were to merely focus on managing the intervals of time between the notes, music would not ensue. Conversely, focusing on the notes alone without attending to the intricate weaving of silences between inspired notes would not result in musicality either. Like a composer, who must balance all three elements—time, notes and rhythms— we must temper activity with stillness, moments of frenzy with moments of quiet contemplation. Only then will we achieve a rhythmic flow in a state of dynamic balance sustained by the melody expressed by our authentic self. Further, you may think of yourself as a note in the collectivity of humans bringing about melodious music in our world, rather than the cacophonic noise that seems to reverberate in the current atmosphere of our culture.

The trouble with "keeping busy"

What I hear most often from people who are retired is that they are now busier than they were during their income-earning years. Sometimes they talk with pride about how well they are "keeping busy." In response to this, I often warn retirees that filling one's days with activities is not necessarily the same as living a life of significance. In the early stages of retirement particularly, an underlying fear may be camouflaged by a constant buzz of plans and activities, many of which serve to fill time, providing entertainment or distraction. Metaphorically, this subconscious fear is akin to falling into the gaping space between scheduled activities if more time were made available. In that gap, huge questions, unfinished business or suppressed emotions may lurk that the retiree does not want to address or feel. By continuing to live at a fast pace, one remains, often unknowingly, on the surface of the waters of life.

"Keeping busy" as a habit may also mean that we jeopardize possibilities of being spontaneous with others in our social life. Friendships tend to become shallow if we must always schedule time with others rather than move with the impulse or need of the moment. Because of our mobility and our excessively scheduled way of life, long gone are the days of "dropping by" unannounced at a relative's or friend's home. Even in your own home environment, "keeping busy" may erode the bonds you have with those closest to you. Without sufficient time for communicating and maintaining closeness, the quality of the relationship will be impoverished. Hence even busy people who appear to have a full social life often go through recurring bouts of loneliness because of the lack of intimacy they experience with others and within themselves. Results of recent research provided at a Be the Change symposium in Vancouver (see resources section) reveal that most adults have only two close friends, and one in four has no one with whom to talk about important matters.

When regrets cloud your mind

Sometimes, the restlessness at the start of retirement or in a hiatus between jobs in midlife may bring some regrets to the surface of your awareness. These could be about missed opportunities, choices you made, or the way you were treated by others at work. Perhaps you will find yourself wishing you had done certain things differently. If regrets are held captive in your mind, it will be more difficult to let go of your past and move forward in the change process leading to new beginnings. On the other hand, some examination of your discontentment can help by pointing you back to the inner compass you may have lost sight of in the busyness of life.

The pain that comes with regrets is in itself a teaching tool as we strive to come to terms with the past and go forward, continuously adjusting our outer life so that it more accurately reflects our core values, our inner life. For some, this pain is experienced with an unbearable intensity particularly when it is felt too late, at the end of one's life. Such was the case for someone I will call Maria, a Portuguese woman who experienced agonizing soul pain at the threshold of her passing.

Tom Maddix, a director of health care at St. Paul's Hospital in Vancouver, B.C., told me the story of this older woman in palliative care at an Edmonton hospital during her last days. At evening time, she denied being physically uncomfortable yet she suddenly began to cry out repeatedly, "Agonia, agonia, agonia," while hitting her chest with her fist. The physician who spoke Portuguese was called to her side. He heard this woman, say she wanted to end her life right there and then. She could not tolerate the agony of realizing time had run out, and she was overwhelmed with regrets about not having fully lived her life.

Perhaps, through her roles and responsibilities, Maria had mostly focused on pleasing others and living up to their expectations while sacrificing much of her own joy. Suddenly, she was in the grip of unbearable anguish as the curtain of consciousness was being drawn, revealing a painful sense of incompleteness about her life. Could it be that she came full circle in time, seeing once again the gifts and the expansive potential that was entrusted to her at birth? This story reminds us that although we may expect to enjoy extended longevity, we had best not waste a moment and we must keep the preciousness of life foremost in mind.

No doubt you have heard that upon approaching life's Grand Finale, we typically do not miss having spent more time at the office or tidying the kitchen at home. In the process of letting go of the past, you are wise to integrate the learning drawn from any regrets you may experience. This assists you to access clarity about what is most important and purposeful to you and to take more responsibility for making the best of each passing moment.

Finding your optimal pace in time

Our society often underestimates the challenges of adapting to retirement, especially if it occurs as result of a company's reorganization or due to cutbacks or layoffs. When our working hours have guided our time allocation and this framework is suddenly or even predictably gone, it takes time to adjust.

Occasionally, when your time is not outwardly structured by work, you may feel drained by a tension between opposing desires and impulses, just below the surface of your awareness. In any given moment, you might sense conflicting demands and wishes, some of which arise from the needs of your inner world versus the needs of your outer world. For example, you may want to be with your grandchild, while also yearning for the tranquility of solitude. Or you may know that you need to walk or somehow exercise today but you find yourself riveted to sedentary activities, such as being at the computer or watching television. Alternatively, you may have much work to do on a project that is driven by a desire to give back, while at the same time noticing that you need to replenish yourself with rest.

In the gateway of retirement, it is important to remember that in such a transition process, one must first come to terms with or let go of the work life you are leaving behind. The middle or neutral zone of this process is characterized by feelings of loss, doubts and fears but also new creative insights. In this phase, we may alternate between feeling depressed and anxious one moment, poised and at peace the next. On the path of renewal, we can befriend the passage of time as we learn to accept the changes we are going through. Think of how time transforms wilting apple blossoms into juicy, ripe fruit on the tree branch.

Those who opt for a gradual or partial retirement usually find it easier to adapt and develop a satisfying, balanced life, with more time available for their personal needs. In contrast to those who are desperate to "keep busy," some retirees who enter retirement "overnight" may move to the opposite end of the spectrum and lose their momentum for an extended period. Men who appeared purposefully focused at work may feel at a loss when they are left to dwell in the time zone of their own personal life. By focusing on the needs of your body, mind and spirit in the interdependence of your family and community, you can nurture a new motivation to be and do what helps you thrive over time.

With adequate support, a balance of activity and rest, and time to reflect while you traverse the transition you are in, you can find your own footing in space and time. In letting go of your previous identification with your professional role and re-awakening to who you are, embracing life more consciously, your relationship with time will naturally change. This process also gives rise to an intrinsic motivation to re-engage yourself in new or continuing endeavors and passions while you develop new relationships that deepen the meaning in your life.

Becoming fully engaged

Intent on restoring your capacity for living in synchronicity with your inner rhythms and renewed purpose you will want to manage your energy, not just your time. In *The Power of Full Engagement*, authors Jim Loehr and Tony Schwartz offer guiding principles to achieve our heart's desires in the context of a vision for optimal living. They explain that to be fully engaged as we manage our energies, not just time, we must draw on four separate but related energy sources. These are the physical, emotional, mental and spiritual realms that are part of each of us.

Among the suggestions contained in *The Power of Full Engagement*, is to recognize the importance of establishing some positive rituals that help to maintain a foundation of values in action from which our life unfolds. Examples of such a ritual could be to reserve time-space for a daily conversation with your partner, for a rejuvenating form of physical activity or for contemplation in a special place in your home. I experience the benefits of such rituals amidst my daily routine. When I start a writing session, for example, I light a candle for inspiration, set the tone with serene music and make my favorite green tea, all of which help to create a space conducive to writing.

Effective ways of establishing what Jon Kabat-Zinn calls a "robust counterbalance in the inner world" to temper the frenzied pace around us include meditation (see chapter 8) and mindfulness practices. Such practices help us to be attuned to our nervous system and oriented toward wisdom-filled states of being, both when we are alone and when we are with others. And when we perceive time and energy as precious, divine gifts, we are inclined to use them in a way that generates a sense of sacredness to what you do.

Although our culture draws us almost seductively into the frenzy and the drama when we are in the midst of difficult circumstances, we can learn to live fully in a new paradigm. To the extent that you refrain from getting overly engaged in momentary challenges, you can better stay attuned to the overall, larger view and direction of your life's unfolding. And by becoming more present to your inner states, attuned to the joy available within and engaged in what you do, you have a positive influence on others.

At this time, one of our collective challenges is to maintain a wider bird's-eye perspective while also keeping a grounded outlook. With this outward-looking but also in-the-moment perspective, our survival instincts converge with our spirit and sacred reverence for nature to provide a deep motivating force. Guided by this force, those of us in midlife and reengagement can be poised in the eternal now, while we help to bring about a livable future for ourselves and those who will follow us.

Questions to ponder

- How do you see your present relationship with time?
- What emotional need in you is calling to be satisfied today?
- What need of others in your life or elsewhere will you seek to respond to today or this week?
- What will you do to restore, maintain or further stimulate your physical energy as part of the lifestyle you are creating now in midlife or in some form of re-engagement?
- What core values are leading your choice of activity today or this week?
- How will you fulfill your need for intellectual stimulation or creativity this week?

CHAPTER 11

Your Financial Resourcefulness

*If you want to feel rich, just count all of
the things you have that money can't buy.*

—Anon

In keeping with one of this book's intentions—to stimulate thinking—
this chapter invites you to be inquisitive about your relationship to
money. How you spend money, what meaning you draw from it, to what extent your happiness is attached to your outer versus your inner wealth are
all worthwhile questions to address.

Given the life span we can now expect, financial sufficiency to last one's
whole life is naturally a concern for many nearing some form of retirement.
Perhaps, like others, you are approaching this transition with a desire to
maintain the lifestyle you have had throughout your working life. Having
sufficient resources for the necessities of life can become a concern when
you are on the threshold of eldership. In the United States particularly, the
soaring costs of health care cause numerous people to worry about secur-
ing adequate medical care as they age.

Aside from this, most people enter retirement wanting to have money to play, travel and enjoy themselves according to their interests and talents. Others also want sufficient funds to begin or continue generative endeavors that reflect their shifting priorities over time. An increasing proportion of those of retirement age find new ways to tap their resourcefulness and to re-engage in their passions while also earning money. Some reinvent themselves with relative ease and create financial flow, but others struggle to develop true financial serenity. As you continue to grow in wisdom, shift your values and acquire tools for managing financial stress, you will also change your relationship to money.

But before examining that relationship, let us explore the powerful "fear of lack," a mindset that can cause many of us to feel caught in cycles of insufficiency at various times in our life.

The virus of insufficiency

It is a recurring theme. "There is not enough!" We say this to each other about money, about time and about possessions. In addition to hearing this from one another, we hear it in the media, spreading bad news about the deteriorating state of the economy. Although we rarely hear about the economy thriving, as it does periodically, we are sure to be told repeatedly when downturns are occurring or about to happen. We must guard ourselves against becoming disturbed by such gloomy news, which can distort our perceptions of our financial reality and our resourcefulness.

In conversation with Lynne Twist, author of *The Soul of Money*, I shared her dismay about our society's widespread perceptions and fears of lack. When do we ever get to decide that we have enough at the present time, let alone for our retirement or re-engagement years? During a workshop I attended called *The Soul of Money* presented by Lynne Twist, she told a story that illustrates to what extent insufficiency can prevail in some people's mind regardless of their circumstances. Having been invited to a private event in New York, Lynne was given the opportunity while there, to share stories of her experiences during her fundraising activities and travels for the Hunger Project. After she spoke that night, Lynne was approached by a man who started the conversation by stating that he was a billionaire, insisting on the "B." He added that for the first time in his life, he had just realized, after hearing her speak, that he has enough money. "Now," said the man, "I want to get into philanthropy." Apparently, even when he was a *millionaire* that man was still caught in the grip of insufficiency. Of course, we do not have to be that wealthy to taste the joys of philanthropy, as demonstrated by the stories in this book.

> *Your wealth will always expand*
> *rather than satisfy your wants.*
> —ANON.

The truth in this quotation reminds us that the more we have, the more we want. Tied to the mindset of "not-enough," a common pattern, which has been particularly encouraged in men, is that of putting all our efforts into work to achieve status and financial wealth. But for some, the insatiable hunger for more often persists, because it is a subconscious compensatory measure for the poverty within. Caught in this cycle we may not realize that we crave to live more authentically and restore more of a balance between our inner and outer life. The middle years and eldership call for us to focus on creating a better equilibrium between having, experiencing, conserving, earning, spending, receiving and giving. At this time, we want to enhance the *qualitative* meaning in our life rather than allowing the *quantitative* aspects to dominate as they may have.

Regardless of the size of your net worth, you may experience angst from time to time about whether or not you have enough money to work less or even retire from remunerated work. This concern could influence major life choices, such as deciding whether to leave or stay in unsatisfying workplaces merely to "pay the bills". During my former job as a social worker, I heard about a man who suddenly died of a heart attack at his retirement party. His colleagues felt sorry for him; they knew this employee had barely endured his last years at work while he so looked forward to his retirement day.

Of course, none of us wishes to end our life this way. A proactive approach is to acknowledge our anxieties around money (and future sufficiency) and confront them in a practical manner. As the next section outlines, there are ways to face and overcome these common fears—without working "till we drop."

Tackling money worries

There is nothing to fear but fear itself.
— FRANKLIN D. ROOSEVELT

Assuredly, the expertise of conscientious financial advisors is invaluable as you assess your needs and calculate how much money you require in preparation for a formal or partial retirement. And you are wise to be discerning about who you select to work with; finding a knowledgeable planner or advisor that shares your value orientation can greatly facilitate the process. However, aforementioned concerns over rising health care needs, unpredictable rates of return on investments, and inflation due to diminishing global resources can all generate anxiety in a long-term planning process. As implied by the quotation above, fear itself can become paralyzing, preventing us from *creating* financial sufficiency rather than merely focusing on finding solutions to financial problems.

A common tendency in the midst of money worries is to shame, blame or punish ourselves while redoubling our efforts to work harder and save more. Yet if we are worried and reactive rather than calm and motivated from within, we risk sinking deeper into anxiety, just as an agitated person can sink deeper in the water and drown. Fortunately, many tools have been developed over the past few years to help us dissolve the stress or accumulated anxiety that keeps some of us in struggling mode. One of these techniques, provided by HeartMath (www.heartmath.org), is called Cut-Thru. It was created to help people gain immediate relief by addressing the perceptions, thoughts and feelings they have around stressful issues.

Once we have cleared the angst we have around money, we can better restore our connection with our ultimate guidance system: the powerful combination of our intuition and our mind. Rather than trying to manipulate ourselves to come up with more *resolve*, we may accept *solutions* to financial challenges that can arise with a sense of ease and flow. Instead of struggling to stay afloat, it is as if we discover the possibility of leaning back on top of the water to float while directing ourselves to our destination. In this state of calm self-directedness, we can better draw upon fresh ideas that may not have otherwise occurred to us if we were nearly in a state of panic.

Practicing gratitude for what we are receiving also helps us release money worries and focuses our mind on what we have rather than what we lack. Since we tend to "get what we focus on," we must be acutely aware of what we give our attention to in order to avoid setting up a negative, self-fulfilling prophecy. Even small practical steps taken toward financial ease can help to shift our attitudes and built better financial results.

In my quest to gain new insights into my own relationship with money, I discovered the book *It's Not About the Money: Unlock your Money Type to Achieve Spiritual and Financial Abundance*, written by the financial planner Brent Kessel. This book explains what Brent calls "financial archetypes. These are like templates of behavioral patterns, beliefs and attitudes that are part of the story we subconsciously formed in relation to money at the core of our psyche—our core story. This core story which I referred to in chapter 5, functions much like the default setting on a computer. Consisting largely of the spoken and unspoken messages we received from our parents, teachers and others, this story forms the paradigm or set of filters through which we see and interpret the world. Identifying all of this helps to better understand the financial life we have, thereby freeing us to live the one we want. To the extent that you become aware of the core story *within* you and also address money matters *without*, you will be more effective as you take charge of your financial life.

From plans to vision

Rather than approaching retirement from a lump sum perspective, a new trend in financial planning is to envision what funds will be needed to achieve core values–driven goals while taking into account possible income-earning capacities. Creating a vision for re-engagement, we become aware of new priorities, one of which may be to simplify our life, thus requiring less income. The current financial picture among boomers is diverse: some have accumulated massive wealth, others are struggling. Some are oblivious of the importance of having savings and sound investments to protect them as they age. They may think financial preparedness reflects an inability to live in the moment or a lack of trust in the all-providing nature of the universe. Certainly, in balance with awareness and mindful actions, trust and faith are part of achieving financial serenity. But for some, the "trust" may actually be a form of denial, a refusal to take responsibility for oneself or to realize that advancing into eldership will eventually lead to a cessation of working income.

Perhaps you are among many in our generation, who expect to enjoy their income-earning life's work for at least a couple more decades. Depending on your state of health and the field in which you work, you may envision earning full-time income into your seventies and beyond. The well-known physician and holistic psychiatrist Abram Hoffer of Victoria, Canada, was still thriving with a full practice in his nineties. But even if such a long career is possible, is it really what you want?

Although some financial advisors may caution you to be "realistic," remember that, aside from tangible aspects of the material world, "reality" is mostly a subjective interpretation of what is. This interpretation, I remind you, is created from how we perceive the world based on the sum total of our cognitive knowledge, our experiences, our attitudes, our beliefs and our expectations. And what is "realistic" for one person may be utterly unrealistic for another. Of course, we must be wise and be prepared for unpredicted events that could cause undue financial strain. But many of us manage to defy the odds, especially when we are driven by the creative life force toward a vision filled with life-affirming purpose and values.

Consider, for example, Rich Henry, whose story is told in chapter 8, who healed against the odds from a cancerous brain tumor. Among numerous other examples, my friend Jan Furst, whom you met in chapter 8, still travels yearly to his native country of Norway. And, was it "realistic" to expect that in his nineties he would also start a sponsorship program for education in Ghana, Africa?

Using money with discernment

When we use our financial resources for what is most meaningful in our lives, our wealth begins to appreciate, and this helps us realize that we actually have enough. I concur with Lynne Twist when she cautions us in her book *The Soul of Money* to avoid hoarding large sums of money because when financial resources are withheld in this way, they tend to become toxic. Money must flow and circulate in order to keep its nourishing vitality, just like the blood in our bodies.

Even when we intend to better appreciate our money and resolve to use it in accordance with our values, we may be unclear at times about distinguishing between our wants and our needs. Because what we perceive as a want versus a need is so intertwined with various unconscious desires, societal pressures and other factors, it can be difficult to discern between the two.

In *It's Not About the Money*, Brent Kessel speaks of the Middle Way as a guide for using discernment and to develop a healthy relationship with money. Long ago, the Indian philosopher Nagurjuna brought forth these teachings based on his mastery of the Middle Way. At the heart of this practice is the concept that a human life has two legitimate goals. The first is to achieve material fulfillment through creation of wealth, and the second is the attainment of liberation through spiritual practice. Importantly, these goals are not mutually exclusive, as some among us in the West may think.

Applying the Middle Way practice to your financial life means that you would steer clear of the reactive behaviors that may be part of your behavioral patterns or derived from your core story. And if you are engaged in a process of spiritual evolution, you will understand that no amount of spending or saving will change the way you feel inside. This is because the inner strengths and resourcefulness that help us to transcend our core story and achieve true serenity do not originate in the material realm but deep within the life force that is part of our human spirit.

On a collective level, spending our money with discernment by being more conscientious consumers can make a sizeable difference in the world around us. When we buy primarily goods and services that are ethically produced and environmentally friendly, we are living up to our social and environmental responsibilities as global citizens. When large numbers of consumers of all generations adopt this discerning approach, harmful products and services eventually disappear. Here is one way we can demonstrate the awareness that collectively, we have the power to vote with our money.

Among those in midlife or entering a partial retirement, a growing number are choosing to use their financial resources to initiate an enterprise. Compelled by their accumulated experience, their renewed passions and sense of purpose, many are contributing products and services in alignment with their most heartfelt values.

The new surge of entrepreneurship

If you are among those ready to unleash your enterprising spirit, you are in good company. Particularly since the 1990s, at least three main factors have converged to help ignite the entrepreneurial flame among those in midlife and beyond. A desire to create their livelihood on their own terms from their own talents and abilities is often the motivating spark. The economic capacity to defray the costs of beginning a business is another factor conducive to embracing entrepreneurship. The third factor is that at all levels of employment, frequent layoffs and downsizing in corporate and government sectors have been eroding the sense of job security many people previously counted on. Hence for these reasons, more among us in midlife or even eldership are motivated to become self-employed.

According to Statistics Canada, between 1990 and 1999, the number of self-employed people aged 45 and older grew by 6.4 percent per year. This continuing trend is particularly strong among women, who are willing to take the necessary risks to venture out on their own or in partnerships. One example, reported by Glen Korstrom in *Business in Vancouver* in August 2006, is the Silk Project. Joanna Staniszkis opened her shop at 62 years of age following a career as a professor in textile design at the University of British Columbia. The idea for her store evolved naturally from her frequent travels around the world to bring back exquisite fabrics she loved. There were difficult moments at the start of her business, she said. But her store is now thriving, attracting those who share her passion for unique objects and stylish wearable art that honor the value of timeless beauty.

Other examples abound of people who have found new or continuing ways to do what they love and earn money at the same time. In the book *Sculpting the Business Body: Strategies and Stories From Top Entrepreneurs*, author Karen McGregor provides a wealth of valuable information derived from her interviews with thirty-seven entrepreneurs, most of whom were in midlife and beyond. Her book includes four pillars of entrepreneurial success and seven thought patterns common to people who prosper with their enterprise.

Among the various new businesses offering goods and services, consultancy is a huge, growing field among boomers and others moving into semi-retirement. As independent consultants or part-time employees, they keep contributing their expertise, wisdom and talent, thus continuing to benefit society. What is more, the insights acquired in the process of reinventing oneself and generating a new livelihood become part of our culture, where they further support innovation and creativity. In addition to the money that many of us continue to earn through various forms of re-engagement, some also expect to receive wealth through the financial legacy of our gradually departing parents.

Indeed, as a generation, boomers in North America are poised to inherit trillions of dollars from their ancestors in the next decade or two. What kind of legacy will we collectively lead with this magnitude of financial resources? What do we want this money to be used for? Aside from wanting a good quality of life, many of us are seeking to get involved in various forms of social entrepreneurship that reflect the greatest commitments of humanity. These commitments are to help create global peace and justice, to protect the environment from further degradation, to end hunger worldwide, and to provide health care and education for all of us on Earth. We must be very thoughtful about how our resources will be saved, bequeathed and transferred to serve not only the best interests of immediate family members but also the greater well-being of our ever-expanding global community.

The next section offers some guidance for wholeheartedly engaging in your new, continuing or renewed life mission. By proactively living forward in this way, you will be joining the visionary leaders of our past and others determined to live to the fullest while helping to build a better world.

Questions to ponder

- What limiting belief, if any, do you hold in mind about having enough money for what you want to be, do and have?
- What is your vision of the lifestyle you plan to have in five, ten or twenty years?
- If you were to more consistently "vote with your money," what would change in the way you spend, allocate or invest your money?
- How are your current core values and needs, including aesthetic and spiritual needs, represented in your budget?

The Dawning of
a New World

CHAPTER 12

The Resurgence of
Visionary Ideals

Ideals are like the stars; we never reach them.
But like the mariners of the sea,
we chart our course by them.

— Carl Schurz

In the context of our responsibilities as members of the human family, the primary focus of this chapter is on the momentous shift toward life-affirming ideals. As well, you will read about some of the factors that hinder our society's progress toward a new vision of humanity. Step with me into the waters of audacity as a keeper of the dream. Like John Lennon, included in chapter 2, "I am not the only one" to insist upon the importance and the power of our collective imagination to hold, to love and to build a better world.

As demonstrated by the thousands of organizations listed in Paul Hawkins's *Blessed Unrest*, more and more people are becoming united in shared purpose, taking courageous actions for a more just and sustainable world. Jeffrey Sachs, among many, comes to mind as a visionary economist who is convinced that extreme poverty can be eradicated. In his best-selling book *The End of Poverty*, Sachs explains that with determination and less than 1 percent of the income of the rich countries, we can reach the goal of preventing people from dying of starvation on this planet. Extreme poverty can become a thing of the past. In spite of the cynicism he encounters and some arguments about corruption undermining aid in many African countries, Sachs is on a mission as if his own life depended on reaching this magnificent goal.

As you will read, ideals to embrace and put into practice are as necessary to our human spirit as the air we breathe. They are imperative to any civilization that is characterized by enduring values and greatness.

Let's get civilized!

When Gandhi visited England in the 1930s he was asked by a journalist: "What do you think of Western civilization?" Gandhi replied: "It would be an excellent idea." Perhaps you wonder, as I do, what he would say about the Western world today. In our complex, high-tech world with its huge interrelated problems, it is unlikely that the West would appear any more "civilized" than it seemed in England in the 1930s.

One of the indicators of a true civilization is that the virtues of civility are flourishing everywhere and its people are caring for their most vulnerable members of society. Rather than spending billions on military budgets, a true civilization would practice the principle of "paying it forward" on a grand scale, to invest in its people and attend to their basic needs. Jeffrey Sachs has pointed out that in 2006, the United States spent $499 billion on its military and only $22 billion on foreign aid. Meanwhile, as Sachs keeps stating about most countries in Africa, "people are dying here, it's an emergency." Even at home in North America, poverty and homelessness are increasing at an alarming rate as the rift between the poor and the rich widens.

Loneliness and isolation are also growing symptoms of our social malaise. With so much automation in our lives we have yet fewer occasions to enjoy an unexpected encounter, share a smile and interact spontaneously with another person for a moment. In large cities, especially, eye contact is becoming increasingly scarce on the streets or in other public places. And too often we silently hunger for direct human contact while sitting alone at our computers.

On the positive side, when technology combines with the collective power of the people, we are able to effect changes that positively impact the whole of humanity. For example, the global campaigning organization Avaaz.org reported in August 2008 that in just over eighteen months their online community had grown to almost 3.4 million. In thirteen languages around the world, these members have taken nearly 8 million actions, including signing petitions, sending messages to leaders, making donations or attending rallies. Ricken Patel of Avaaz stated, "We've started to win real victories to close the gap between the world we have and the world we want—on human rights, environmental protection, poverty, global justice and more." Two of the group's recent achievements were to raise over $2 million in aid after the 2008 Burma cyclone and to effectively pressure world leaders to agree on a firm treaty to ban cluster bombs at an international summit.

While we appreciate the far-reaching impact technology can have, we also need to guard against worshiping technology, allowing it to run our lives or shape our minds. In *A Whole New Mind*, Daniel Pink argues that our left-brain functions are increasingly being taken over by our high-tech world. Conversely, the good news, for those of us who are predominantly right brain-oriented, is that aptitudes of holistic thinking, synthesis and creativity are becoming more highly valued. These are the right-brain functions that cannot be replaced by technology as we strive to find new solutions in our ailing world. Especially at this critical time, we must not underestimate the value of our human aptitudes or allow ourselves to be infected by the virus of speed and excessive pragmatism.

Challenging excessive pragmatism, dualism and cynicism

In *The Heart Aroused: Poetry and the Preservation of the Soul in Corporate America*, David Whyte writes about work as the place that "feeds the enormous human need for getting things done." If work is all about *doing*, says Whyte, the soul is all about *being*. It is the "indiscriminate enjoyer" and witness of everything that comes our way. Whyte encourages us to restore our connection with our soul to counteract the effects of living in our increasingly pragmatic, doing-oriented world.

One indicator of this pragmatism is that how-to books are now everywhere, providing instructions on how to do just about anything. Though many of these books are valuable, their genre reflects our increasing insistence on wanting to follow a direct, preferably short, logical method. In many cases, we are too impatient to take on a process that engages our intuition, our own creativity and courage as well as our cognitive faculties. Having come to count on vast information banks such as the Internet, many of us rely on quick answers that are just a few clicks away. The hectic pace of our culture also contributes to our diminishing tolerance for process and our corresponding urges to achieve fast, direct outcomes as often as possible.

In our haste to get to quick results, we can overlook the benefits of proceeding organically rather than mechanically. This is a way that taps the holistic, intuitive intelligence built into our instincts, not just our logical mind. What is more, the habit of rushing to solutions or focusing on problems can become a diversion from actually creating what we really want.

As Robert Fritz points out in *The Path of Least Resistance: Learning to Become the Creative Force in Your Own Life*, "there is a profound difference between problem solving and creating. Problem solving is taking action to have something go away—the problem. Creating is taking action to have something come into being." In his book, Fritz explains the implications of these different approaches for our world collectively and individually.

Given society's current disproportionate emphasis on practicalities, the numinous and mythical dimensions that give depth to our life are also devalued. We end up even being estranged from the desire to know these dimensions in ourselves.

> *Mythology is the wellspring of our civilization.*
> — DEEPAK CHOPRA

Just as most children seek to know where they come from—what is God and what heroes they could admire—as a culture evolves, its members go through the same questioning. The myths passed down by ancestors hold answers about our origin, about universal truths and other questions that typically inhabit our psyche. Through time, mythic tales have also provided guidance for negotiating the forces of light and darkness in ourselves. But now, our overly pragmatic modern society is increasingly devoid of mythology that can serve as a frame of reference and offer a worldview within which to position ourselves.

As the author Michael Meade stated, "While nature rattles and culture unravels, mythic imagination tries to return to the world and awaken a meaningful purpose and helpful direction in each person's life." Meade's new book *The World Behind the World* is a guide for living "at the ends of time." It is an introduction to "living myth" that involves the reimagination of culture at all levels. Meade helps us understand to what extent myth is important in making meaning and in supporting each person to find meaningful practices and paths for life.

Deep down, in midlife especially, we often long to reach for that dimension that is larger than ourselves, just as flowers naturally turn toward sunlight. Staying connected with the wholeness within also prevents us from becoming fragmented or from taking on a dualistic way of seeing the world.

Dualism contributes to our habit of categorizing things and people as, simply put, good or bad. It keeps our mind occupied with judging everything we come across. And we judge things at such speed that we do not even realize it most of the time. Under the influence of technology, we are now even more likely to justify this judging habit because we do it daily, perhaps thousands of times, by the click of our computer mouse. And our decision to delete, keep or select is made increasingly faster by necessity, given the huge amounts of information and numbers of e-mail we must sort through daily. To be efficient at this task, we are constantly training ourselves to eliminate all ambiguity from our thinking. In the complexity of our daily life, which demands quick judgments and unequivocal decisions, dualism may simplify our lives. But the totality of such judgments and the multiple shallow communications we engage in daily contribute to render our mind more simplistic and judgmental. Hence we tend to become less relational with one another and we prefer to read, or be told or shown, about "how to" accomplish what we must.

In a new humanity, the dualism in our minds would give way to a courageous encounter with the wholeness of things and people as they are. While we refrain from denying or struggling against negative forces, we can learn from adversity and lean toward what supports life. Scott Peck reminds us, in a chapter entitled "The Evils of Compartmentalization" in the anthology I co-authored, *Einstein's Business: Embracing Soul, Imagination and Excellence in the Workplace*, "the crux of integrity is wholeness." He adds that the co-existence of good and evil is a paradox we must embrace in order to live our lives with integrity.

If we can lessen our habits of judging, categorizing or believing all of our thoughts, we might better appreciate the paradox of our diversity in the midst of the oneness we share. Rather than harboring a mindset of relative mistrust of others, we would focus on their strengths, thereby drawing forth the best from one another. In that quality of presence, without prejudging, we could trust our experiences of whom and what we encounter, then respond or act according to our intuitive signals, our knowledge and our resourcefulness. By adopting a more inclusive, holistic mindset, we can temper our dualistic tendencies. Another habit calling to be extinguished is cynicism.

Wherever it turns up, cynicism seems to be the antithesis of generosity, often indicating a loss or lessening of our innate appreciation for beauty, innocence and ideals. Insidious in its influence, the virus of cynicism tends to develop as a defense, a sort of hardening against the vulnerability that comes with living from heart-centered values. This shadow is also commonly found in those who become bitter as a result of focusing almost exclusively on problems and limitations rather than on creating out of potential and possibilities.

Whether permeating the hallways of a workplace, lingering at staff meetings or infusing the culture of a company, cynicism erodes possibilities of openness with its pernicious and toxic effect. Pervasive in its effect, cynicism engenders a collusion that pressures people to join in and adopt that way of thinking and communicating, thereby jeopardizing trust in the workplace. Even rugged individualists may find it difficult to resist the pressure because deep down, we all want an experience of belonging to the organization that we invest ourselves in day after day.

Beyond the workplace, cynicism also shows up in various social settings and occasionally within a family. Perhaps you have witnessed a relative slowly abandoning one of their dreams and gradually becoming bitter. Each time someone gives up an aspiration previously held close to their heart, the energy and the light dims within them. Those around them may feel pulled downward toward a kind of darkness. It is as if an anchor has been dropped into murky waters, and a negative, stagnant atmosphere descends upon the family.

In spite of the various disappointments we have experienced by the time we get to midlife, practicing curiosity, kindness and openness can bridge the gap between our current reality and the one we want to reach for. On a very personal level, recovering one's innocence and dreams also means that we shed lingering traces of feeling undeserving of goodness and happiness. As a generation, shifting away from cynicism and shedding our collective guilt for what has been blamed on us will help us move forward into generative and restorative actions. We must also guard against allowing shades of cynicism to extinguish the spark of enthusiasm and idealism that is typically present in the younger generations.

Ideals: Stepping stones toward our desired Future

No society can endure without the sense of honour, dignity
and transcendence enshrined in its sets of ideals.
—JOHN O'DONOHUE.

In *Beauty: The Invisible Embrace*, O'Donohue explains compellingly that ideals awaken a sense of passion and urgency in us, to reach beyond our limitations toward excellence and beauty. When we reach for the best in ourselves, we are also more likely to invite something new and surprising to unfold from within. On a personal level, when we have excellence as one of our core values and priorities, we find more joy and satisfaction from whatever we do.

I once met a taxi driver who was in his middle years and seemed to harbor resentments about his perceived lack of career opportunities. As a contrary example, I recall hearing about a remarkable taxi driver who was providing the ultimate, courteous service with a choice of coffee and newspapers available in his vehicle. He loved his work because he had transcended its predictable, routine-like aspect by becoming an excellent, outstanding driver who amazed every one of his clients.

Ideals such as truth, beauty, honor and harmony with nature are supported by our imagination. They can lead us to a keen awareness of what it means to be a whole human being, to learn, grow and love. Ideals are like the True North on our collective compass, while the arrow is the convergence of our intentions and actions pointing toward our sets of ideals. Yet we know that when we try to keep the arrow rigidly in place pointing to some narrow point or standard, idealism may turn into fanaticism.

Throughout history, many cultures and religious groups have taken what was initially an inspiring set of values and turned it into a moral code, a constrictive dogma in which everyone is pressured to conform. This seems to occur when ideals are being dictated by zealots rather than arising from the heart or from the core of our collective human spirit. The rise of fundamentalism, expressed as holy wars or repressive rules of conduct in various areas of the world, is an increasing threat at this time. Given the fears associated with religious fanaticism, the West has seen growing trends of secularism spreading across their institutions. But pushed to extremes, secularism can inadvertently lead us to be even more estranged from our spirituality and from the light of ideals, thus intensifying our fragmentation and widespread crisis of meaning.

In *Beauty: The Invisible Embrace*, John O'Donohue speaks of beauty as an essential nourishment to the soul. Like him, I believe we all share a deep yearning for beauty. I personally seek it in nature, in choosing what surrounds me, in the clothes I wear, and in the art I create. Beauty imparts a feeling of harmony that is soothing to the soul, especially in our chaotic and confusing times. In an e-mail exchange, my friend Hugo Ateo offered a keen insight into beauty when he wrote: "It's amazing how beauty responds to appreciation by growing, refining itself, widening its field of influence and pervading everything it touches." Perhaps you have noticed when beauty arises in someone you particularly appreciate. When a friend or one of my children says or does something that reveals an openness and luminosity shining up from the heart, I am moved by their beauty.

But while we hunger for beauty, this intangible mysterious ideal, there seem to be fewer ways for us to witness it in our Western world. Our increasing focus on practicalities and need for speed are now countering our previous enthusiasm toward beauty. Art's primary purpose used to be expressing and celebrating beauty and serving our yearning for aesthetics. Gradually, over the past decades, art has come to be valued mostly as a mode of self-expression. This enables everyone to enter artistic endeavors for the pleasure of expressing themselves and their unique interpretations of the world.

Yet while valuing self-expression is a wonderful way to honor each other's uniqueness, the current products of artistic endeavors are not always aesthetically pleasing. Those who are called to express beauty through art might find the present trends not particularly conducive to what they yearn to create. For example, I once heard an art student lament that his talent for depicting the beauty of nature or of the human body in a painting was unappreciated, even seen as passé. Thus, collectively, we are left with fewer possibilities of being moved or embraced by beauty. Nature, of course, remains masterful at offering its beauty to our eyes. And this is one of the reasons we must allow ourselves to be fully in love with the Earth: for its exquisite beauty and all of the ways our existence depends on it.

Embracing the spirit of interdependence

In a civilization modeled after timeless ideals, the interdependence that binds us all would be manifested in the way we care for one another. But our individualistic culture fosters the belief that each person is solely responsible for all of their current circumstances. Taken to extremes, this belief can make us morally irresponsible. Surely our attitudes, our beliefs and our self-concept account for much of what we repel, attract or create, yet other forces also affect us that are beyond the realm of our individual influence. As our collective consciousness expands, we are naturally inclined to cultivate humility and practice compassion in response to the interdependent nature of humanity.

Through multiple scientific experiments as well as our intuitive or spiritual knowing, more and more of us realize that we are all affecting one another in many more ways than meet the eyes. A stunning example of this was reported in *Shift* magazine in June-August 2007. In an article titled "The Power of the Collective," quantum physicist John Hagelin summarizes the study he conducted in 1993 in Washington, D.C. A large number of meditation practitioners assembled in the area during the summer months, which are typically associated with a strong surge of violent crime. With the collaboration of the FBI, criminologists and social scientists, amazing results were revealed after the group of daily meditators reached 2,500. Suddenly, as Hagelin reports, "There was a distinct and highly statistically significant drop in crime compared to expected rates based on previous data, weather conditions, and a variety of other factors." These tangible results provide documented evidence for the interconnectedness between us.

When the Buddhist monk, activist and author Thich Nhat Hanh promotes an understanding of interdependence around the world, he often uses a biological metaphor. He speaks of organic living in which people around our planet would learn to live as an organism, much as the trillions of cells in all the diverse parts of the body collaborate toward the well-being of the whole. Just imagine, for a moment, what that could be like!

Stewardship of the Earth: An invitation to sustainability

At the most fundamental level, stewardship means we meet our sacred responsibility to love and care for our home planet and its inhabitants in recognition that spirit resides in everything. Across all generations and especially among those in midlife and eldership, people are responding to the call of being stewards of the Earth in various ways. Be the Change, Awakening the Dreamer, and Change the Dream symposiums are examples of the many programs being offered to citizens in multiple locations across America and other continents. Through these programs, participants are inspired to take a stand for an environmentally sustainable, personally meaningful and socially just human presence on this planet. These events also provide opportunities for grassroots groups to form and take action to become stewards as they support one another into being the Change we urgently need. In community with others at such events, participants recognize the profound interconnection between all beings as they also identify some erroneous assumptions that led us to the present environmental crisis. "Throwing away" something disposable is an example of assumptions misleading us to think that things magically disappear once "thrown away."

The world-renowned scientist and environmentalist David Suzuki sees the possibilities of avoiding this ecological catastrophe when he states that sustainability can be achieved if we learn to live within the Earth's limits. In the long term, this includes being able to tackle the root causes of health and environmental problems before they occur. In the report *Sustainability within a Generation*, written for the David Suzuki Foundation, David R. Boyd outlines a workable plan that would allow Canada to lead the way toward achieving sustainability.

Although social changes are rapid with respect to understanding the magnitude of our environmental crisis, some people manage to keep such concerns out of their mind by stating that they are not "environmentalists." Yet every breath we take is an expression of an intimate relationship with our environment. Fortunately, virtually everyone is waking up to the unequivocal evidence of global warming and all of its mounting effects. We are now seeing prominent people calling us to respond by taking action, changing our habits and simplifying our lifestyle. *This Moment on Earth*, a book by the Massachusetts senator John Kerry and Teresa Heinz Kerry, is among many examples of the current focus on the urgency of our global crisis.

The conversation-in-action movement

> *As the self is repatterned, the ways we relate to each other are necessarily shifting as well, toward the discovery of new styles of interpersonal connection and new ways of being in community, given a global society.*
> — JEAN HUSTON

Among the "new ways of being in community," various models of conversation have arisen. From World Café created by Juanita Brown to Circles of Trust developed by Parker Palmer and Wisdom Council conversations, we now have many more opportunities to invoke spiritually intelligent solutions together. This phenomenon influences the culture of organized meetings; learning from people's wisdom and experience is getting to be valued perhaps as much and sometimes more than advice and information from "experts." As well, when we use diversity and inclusiveness as guiding values, we are en route to finding workable solutions that correspond to the common concerns and issues we share. Together, in community, we also produce collective intelligence that is greater than that of any individual.

Opportunities are now multiplying, literally "as we speak," for us to courageously contribute our personal leadership to keep this movement in motion. Conversations among us help to grow a new grassroots kind of democracy and feed the spirit of global citizenship that must prevail for us to thrive as a species. As individual sparks and flames ignite into fire, every focused conversation that connects us together in action feeds the growing movement for change, thereby accelerating the shift we need to bring about the Future.

Getting together to enrich our culture and civilization with poetry, song, art and inspiration is also important. If, in our hectic pace and survival mode, we come to focus exclusively on the pragmatic, we become further fragmented and out of balance, severed from our wisdom and our inner life force. In order to restore the balance in our collective soul, and in nature, we must come together beyond the mechanistic dealings and transactions through which we merely get things done.

Guided by an ancient African teaching, "We make the road by walking," Doug Cohen has developed, in the United States, the Inspired Futures Campaign, a mentoring and learning journey committed to fostering youth leadership and sustainability. Doug told me that his work "has ranged widely from the direct personal experience of teaching and mentoring hundreds of emerging leaders to building systemic coalitions with organizations and colleagues on behalf of large-scale sustainability education initiatives." One of the young women touched by the Inspired Futures Campaign, Marisa Guber, wrote the following:

> I feel blessed to be a proactive member of a growing intergenerational movement that is working towards creating a healthy world. While completing an MA in Socially Responsible Business and Sustainable Communities and working in the field, I have seen the principles put into action as innovations drive creative solutions that honor the planet and its people. Although there are many challenges, I draw inspiration from this multi-faceted movement that is rooted in interdependence, connectivity and shared learning among global citizens.

At the intersection of spirituality and sustainability, Doug Cohen is now developing an institute to bridge the gap between spiritual and environmental leadership, and to address sustainability challenges for the whole of humanity.

Ways of perceiving our tomorrows

Over the past decades our generation has instigated and witnessed scientific revelations that transformed our relationship with the world. The physicist David Bohm, who worked with Albert Einstein, found that "thought creates the world" long before the New Age movement promoted this idea. In his book *Wholeness and the Implicate Order*, Bohm explains the theory of the implicate order, which is the unmanifested level of reality. Albert Einstein asserted that "the world we have created is a product of our way of thinking." It follows that when each and every one of us changes our thinking, we are changing the world. In 1990 Vaclav Havel, then the president of Czechoslovakia, affirmed the importance of shifting our consciousness when he stated: "Without a global revolution in the sphere of human consciousness, nothing will change for the better . . . and the catastrophe toward which this world is headed—the ecological, social, demographic or general breakdown of civilization—will be unavoidable."

In an article entitled "A World Shaped by Choice," published in the anthology *Living the Questions*, Peter M. Senge guides us into three distinct ways that we can think about our future. First there's the "extrapolation" model, in which we simply see the future as an extension of the present and recent past. Another way to think of it is by taking a leap of imagination that takes us entirely away from the influence of the present on the future. A third way is by cultivating an exquisite presence and awareness, to be open to what is arising and what wants to manifest through us and in our world. From that awareness, we then seek to "align human intentions and actions with the course of nature," says Senge.

The kind of thinking required now is not based on blind trust in human ingenuity, which often assumes that we can find our way out of whatever problems we created. Rather, this way of seeing the future requires that we trust in the nature of life itself and in our ability to tap the greater realm of intelligence, the Grand Will, as we become a force of nature, as Peter Senge suggests. And in the field of the collective unconscious, we can join in spirit those, such as Martin Luther King Jr., Mother Teresa and Ghandi, who were "forces of nature" who changed our world forever.

In the next chapter, you will meet women who have aligned their human intentions and actions with the course of nature while they help to usher in the Future we want.

Questions to ponder

- Which ideals do you want to embrace more wholeheartedly in your daily life? And how would your life be different if you were to do so?
- How can you foster the spirit of interdependence in your community or perhaps in your workplace?
- What changes can you make in your daily life to better participate in the stewardship of the Earth?
- What new community conversations would you like to be a part of?
- What is your perception of how the future will come about in relation to our past history?

CHAPTER 13

Women Ushering in the Future

The future of the world depends on women.

— Kofi Annan

More than any other time in recent history, women are now stepping
forward, demonstrating their ability to lead, to excel in numerous
fields of endeavor and to connect with others through caring actions. In the
past few years, I have met, mostly at conferences, many outstanding women
who might say they are ordinary women. Yet something moves them beyond ordinariness into living lives of profound significance. I believe what
drives them is their heart-centered commitment to continue innovating, to
lead with their insights, and to contribute their generosity of spirit toward
the betterment of our world.

In addition to the remarkable women you already met in this book,
seven women are featured here as pioneers helping to bring about a more
desirable future. Clearly, a whole book could be written about each of these
women; I offer only a snapshot of each one's achievements and their way of
being gifts to the world. These women are Marcia Jaffe, Betty Williams,

Linda Dunkel, Margaret Wheatley, Lynne Twist, Myriam Laberge and Maureen Jack-Lacroix. Information about their organizations is included in the resources section.

Regardless of your gender, as you read I hope you will be inspired or feel affirmed in your values and in your own unique manner of contributing. And if you are among those who wholeheartedly participated in the rise of feminism back in the seventies, you may wonder what has happened to this movement among women. A brief exploration of a third wave of liberation is included here as well a glimpse of the many faces of philanthropy among women today.

Marcia Jaffe: Learning from the people of Bali

You read, in chapter 9, an account of what happened when Marcia went to Bali for a vacation in 2003. I initially met her in Bali in 2004 at the first Quest for Global Healing conference, which she organized with her colleagues Wilford Welch and Carole Angermier. I feel particularly grateful toward them for having created this event, which has made a significant difference in the course of my life.

When Marcia spoke in Ubud, Bali, at this first conference, I could hear the full strength of her love for the Balinese culture and its people. I sensed that to create this magnificent event, Marcia and her colleagues had devoted countless hours of hard work and determination to bring their vision into reality.

A second Quest for Global Healing was held in 2006, also in Bali, which drew more than 650 people from over 30 countries. This time, a first Global Youth in Action program was part of the event. It was particularly moving for me to see a great sampling of young people from around the world, eager to inspire and to contribute their energy, infused with ideals held in their hearts. Global visionary leaders were part of this conference as well. These included three Nobel Peace Prize laureates—Archbishop Desmond Tutu, Betty Williams and Jody Williams—and the *Apollo 14* astronaut Edgar Mitchell (the sixth man to walk on the Moon), Bhutan's Minister of Culture the Honorable Lyonpo Jigmi Thinley, Afghanistan's Red Crescent Society president, and numerous others.

In a recent conversation, Marcia and I talked about our admiration for the values embraced by the Balinese. The honoring of their spirituality and their interconnectedness in thoughts and actions are among the values predominant in Bali, in sharp contrast to what prevails in the West.

Marcia shared a story she heard from her son Ryan Feinstein, as an example of how the Balinese live up to their values. Ryan, who helped to organize the conferences, was on a boat in Bali talking with a Balinese man, asking him about his dreams. The man replied that he wanted to go work on a cruise ship to earn more money for his family. He explained that a payment of $2,000 is required for the training and to become an employee on a cruise ship. Not long before this conversation, the Balinese man had accumulated this amount, after four years of saving. But then a person in his village became ill and the money was given to the family for the medical care of their sick relative. "But I still have my dream," said the man with a sparkle in his eye.

Following this account, Marcia said to me, "I'll never forget this story!" and she remembers noticing how much it touched her son by the look on his face when he told her the story. This is but one vivid example of the interdependence that infuses the way of life in Bali, which compels Marcia and her team to do all they can to help people from the West to learn from the Balinese. Like Marcia, I believe the integration of this spirit of oneness in our world is necessary for us all to sustain our continuity on the planet.

Early in 2008, Marcia and her colleagues launched the Bali Institute for Global Renewal, which further brings together world leaders and global citizens from around the world to learn together and to be positively influenced by the indigenous culture of Bali.

Betty Williams: Upholding the rights of children

At the second Quest for Global Healing event in Bali in 2006, I had the opportunity to meet Betty Williams when I was one of the conference volunteers. When she spoke at this event, I recall noticing that her words conveyed a firm resolve and deep commitment to her cause and her projects aimed at relieving the immense suffering of children in war-torn countries. Because of my own background in social work and child protection, I was particularly moved by her devotion to caring for these precious members of our global family.

Along with Mairead Corrigan, Betty Williams was awarded the Nobel

Peace Prize in 1976 for her work to bring peace in her native Northern Ireland. Since that time, she has dedicated herself to creating nothing less than a movement to change how we deal with the injustices, cruelty and horror perpetrated on the world's children.

> *Thirty years in the field has convinced me of one thing, the*
> *obvious fact that there are no answers from the top down.*
> *Governments do not have the answers. Indeed quite the reverse.*
> *A lot of times they not only do not have the answers, they*
> *themselves are the problem. If we are committed to helping*
> *our world's children, then we must begin to create solutions*
> *from the bottom up.* — BETTY WILLIAMS

Betty Williams has traveled the globe to listen to and record the testimonies of children subjected to horrors beyond belief. She soon realized that legislation to protect children must be implemented to persuade governments to hear their children and acknowledge their basic rights. From this work, Betty Williams was compelled to create centers of compassion and peace to ensure that children at risk are treated lovingly and with the dignity and respect they deserve.

After many years of hard work, Betty Williams founded the Global Children's Studies Center in 1992. This evolved into her founding the World Centers of Compassion for Children International (WCCCI) in 1997, in honor of His Holiness the Dalai Lama. Betty Williams's remarkable devotion resulted in her receiving nearly twenty prestigious honors and awards, among them, the Martin Luther King Jr. Award and the Eleanor Roosevelt Award. Betty Williams is also the author of *Madness in My Country*, and as of September 2008 was working on another book.

Linda Dunkel, tireless humanitarian

On a long flight to Bali for the second Quest for Global Healing conference, I had the good fortune to meet Tony Dunkel and his wife, Linda Dunkel. Seated next to each other, Linda and I conversed at length and later shared that we experienced one another as kindred spirits. Linda is president and chief executive officer of Interaction Associates (IA). This outstanding company empowers people in organizations and communities to realize their most noble aspirations by demonstrating the skills and the power of collaborative action.

When Linda spoke at the 2006 conference about ways to be personally and professionally aligned with our values, I sensed she was speaking from a place of deep integrity. She is an outstanding model of congruence, as evidenced by her many achievements, including her collaborative leadership in running this unique forty-year-old firm, IA. Linda believes in conscious capitalism and operates the firm in this socially conscious way. One example is that in 1993, Interaction Associates became the first firm of its kind to fund a nonprofit institute, the Interaction Institute for Social Change. Not surprisingly, Linda was named one of America's Best Bosses in November 2006 by the nonprofit organization Winning Workplaces.

Since we met, I remained in contact with the Dunkels and had the pleasure of seeing them again in 2007 in Bali. I heard then that Linda, Tony and their daughter Stacy had been playing major roles in the development of the WCCCI, founded by Betty Williams. When Linda spoke in Bali in 2007, she mentioned that she had been extending herself to be of service by simply and frequently asking, "How can I help?" She also assisted the audience to understand the steps for leading one's vision to fruition. Begin by envisioning what you want to bring about, she said, then "pressure-test" your vision with your own personal "board of directors" and articulate your vision compellingly to others, in a way that engages collaborative action.

Especially since she entered midlife, Linda has become a tireless humanitarian through her work with women's and girls' organizations and refugee groups to help children globally. She is now chair of the board of WCCCI and her daughter Stacy Dunkel, also an advocate for the rights of children, is the vice-president of operations of WCCCI–US.

If the Future could speak, it would express gratitude to Linda for being on its front line, wholeheartedly active, leading a life of compassion in action and embodying loving integrity.

Margaret Wheatley and the Berkana Institute

"Whatever the Question, Community is the Answer" was the title of an article that caught my attention in 2005 about the author, consultant and internationally acclaimed speaker Margaret Wheatley. While she was in Vancouver for her presentation that year, I invited her to contribute to the anthology *Einstein's Business*, which I had just initiated with a publishing company in California. She later provided a wonderful chapter for that book which includes her poem called "Action," an excerpt of which follows:

> Action, like a sacrament, is the visible form of an invisible spirit
> An outward manifestation of an inward power.
> But as we act, we not only express what is in us and help give shape to the world.
> We also receive what is outside us and we reshape our inner selves.
> When we act, the world acts back.
> And we and the world are co-created.

One of the many ways Margaret Wheatley manifests *her* inward power is through her work in Africa and with the Berkana Institute she founded. This institute connects and supports life-affirming leaders around the world who strengthen their communities by working with the wisdom and wealth already present in its people and in the environment. You may recall reading in chapter 4 the story of Janey Talbot, whose life was transformed as a result of her participation in one of the institute's Learning Journeys in Africa.

In April 2008 I was again inspired and informed by Margaret's presentation in Vancouver at a Women's Leadership Revival event. That evening she provided startling statistics about the gender inequalities and economic injustices that still prevail, particularly in the developing countries. She told the audience that worldwide, 65 percent of the work is currently done by women while they receive 5 percent of the resources. Furthermore, 70 percent of all women are illiterate and one-third of all women suffer from domestic abuse. Meanwhile, much of the resources of the G-8 countries are allocated to "defense"—and offence—budgets, with over $1 trillion being spent on military budgets yearly.

Margaret reminds us that when women achieve economic means, local economies prosper, children thrive and everyone benefits. Kofi Annan's words back her up, as quoted in *Ode* magazine in May 2008: "If there is one lesson we in the United Nations have learned over the years, it is that investing in women is the most productive strategy a country can pursue." This is so because women use their resources to care for their families and their homes and to educate their children, who in turn will later have more income-earning possibilities.

In one of her most recent books, *Finding Our Way: Leadership for an Uncertain Time*, Margaret Wheatley urges us all to rely on our human goodness and creativity to *find our way* to the changes needed for our time. She points out that the current conditions in our world fail to bring about the best in humans and that women are instrumental in creating conditions conducive to the fundamental shift urgently required. Like her, as I indicated by this chapter's title, I believe that women are better positioned than ever before to usher in the desirable Future we all want.

Lynne Twist: Learning from indigenous peoples

When I watched the video series *Women of Power and Wisdom*, created and directed by Lili Fournier several years ago, I was deeply touched by Lynne Twist, who is among those featured in this inspiring series. Still now, when I see Lynne speak about leading "a committed life" with such humility and love for humanity, I feel moved and validated in my desire to keep committing my heartfelt values into purposeful action.

I met Lynne when I attended her transformative Soul of Money workshop in 2004 and again at several other conferences in the past few years. Her book *The Soul of Money* was mentioned several times in other chapters. The mission of The Soul of Money Institute she founded in 2003 is to inspire, educate and empower people to realign the acquisition and allocation of financial resources with their most deeply held values. The timely themes of her institute for 2008, as stated in her newsletter, are "the indomitable human spirit resilient to the ups and downs of market forces and the celebration of sufficiency (we have enough, do enough, and are enough)."

Lynne is also the co-founder, with her husband Bill Twist, of the Pachamama Alliance, whose mission is twofold: to preserve the Earth's tropical rainforest by empowering the indigenous people who are its natural custodians, and to contribute to the creation of a new global vision of equity and sustainability for all.

In 2008, Lynne and Bill were living and working full-time in Ecuador to participate in important historic events occurring there. One current breakthrough is that, supported by his population, the new president of Ecuador, Rafael Correa, is in conversations with selected global experts to draft a new constitution that will integrate the rights of the Earth and all species in fundamental constitutional law.

Knowing as we do that the Earth's tropical rainforests are part of the lungs of our planet, the work of the Pachamama Alliance is of great importance at this crucial time. The Alliance offers several trips yearly to the Amazonian Rainforests providing the opportunity to be in direct contact with the Echuar—an ancient people in the early stages of their relationship with the modern world. I hope to go on this life-changing journey myself, to experience untouched stands of tropical rainforest and to learn about living in harmony with the Earth from the elders and shamans in this culture. Paradoxically, it seems that our best future is contingent on, among other things, retrieving the wisdom from the past, when humanity was living in harmony with nature. Hence Lynne and Bill Twist's work through the Alliance is not only imperative in terms of the preservation of nature, but it is also a bridge to the profound spiritual relationship with the Earth that resides in the Echuar people.

Myriam Laberge: Facilitating important conversations

After Myriam Laberge heard a poem I shared with the audience at a networking meeting in Vancouver in 2005, she introduced herself to me and our friendship began to grow immediately. Getting to know Myriam was like opening a treasure chest of skills, talents and character strengths. A senior management and organization development consultant, facilitator and educator, Myriam has been the president and co-founder of Breakthroughs Unlimited Inc. since 1990. She particularly loves to work with whole systems on the organizational level in the private, public and social profit worlds, to bring about transformative change and creative solutions to complex issues.

Myriam is a remarkable model of what it means to align who we are with what we do. Embracing a love for her country, Myriam was summoned to create opportunities for ordinary Canadians to have a voice in the future of Canada during the difficult period of the 1995 Quebec referendum. This engagement resulted in her being named to the 1996 *Maclean's* magazine honor roll. In 1996, she was an Ethics in Action Award nominee for her leadership and contribution to grassroots participation in the category of Canadian Unity, for her People-to-People Search for Canada initiative.

In 2007 she co-led, with Brenda Chaddock, a retreat called Facilitating Wise Action for Lasting Impact on Bowen Island, near Vancouver. There I experienced her passion for igniting the spirit of collective intelligence and wisdom through dialogue. When we talked recently about this, she said, "I've come to know that magic can happen in groups, releasing extraordinary potential, goodwill and creativity." She added: "Tapping collective intelligence and wisdom usually requires an investment of time spent together in dialogue—sharing, exploring, discovering, learning, bridging, dreaming and planning. Also, a deeply compelling question must catalyze the group's central intention." As I myself observed, Myriam is masterful at providing the appropriate process for such dialogue and at establishing a foundation of respect and civility among members in conversations. Then the magic can appear, spark co-creative genius, and unite people in their shared intentions to be wiser and better human beings together.

Myriam strongly believes in the imperative of providing opportunities for people to be involved together in meaningful conversations around questions that matter to them. These community dialogues are part of the equation of what it takes for us all to become fully actualized individuals while we collectively help to bring about a better future.

Maureen Jack-Lacroix: Dedicated to service and social change

It was at a gathering for members of the Institute for Noetic Science in Vancouver in 2007 that I first met Maureen. I was immediately struck by her gentle yet outspoken way of interacting and by her glowing face framed by silver curls. Maureen is one of those women with many talents flowing into a few areas of endeavor expressive of an underlying soul purpose. In addition to her roles as event producer, workshop leader and executive business coach, Maureen is the founding director of Be the Change Earth Alliance.

On her 50th birthday, Maureen declared her pledge to devote the next decade of her life to be of service to the Earth. She then set about to close her lucrative production company, complete her master's degree in creation spirituality and eco-psychology (through Naropa University) and settle into the core of her life's purpose. A spirit of service has run through her past few decades, as evidenced by her being honored with the Exceptional Contribution Award from UNICEF Canada in 1985 and the *Ethics In Action Award* from the Vancouver's Workplace Ministry Society and the credit union Vancity in 1996.

When I attended a Be the Change symposium in Vancouver in 2008, I saw Maureen's leadership in action. There she effectively engaged and inspired the participants in collaborative approaches to social change and sustainable lifestyles. Through that day, she instigated among all the attendees a sense of inquisitiveness; of wanting to look within and ponder what is required of us now. Like me, Maureen believes in the necessity of asking ourselves important questions. One of those started to germinate in her when she came upon this quotation from the late R. Buckminster Fuller: "If success or failure of this planet and of human beings depended on how I am and what I do, how would I be? What would I do?"

Taking this inquiry to heart, Maureen has come to embody her ecological values while she contributes to co-creating the shift in consciousness we are called to make: from "me" to "we." "This global mind shift is truly ego-shattering," she says. "Because of how humbling it is to face the enormity of the tasks of combating global warming, we come to realize that *I* cannot solve this problem, but *we* can." Maureen encourages concerned citizens to join Be the Change circles, use the action guides provided, and give each other the peer support we all need to shed old habits and make new lifestyle choices that spark significant change. Fostering the spirit of interconnectedness in our society is clearly one of the ways that she is indeed helping to bring a better future into reality.

Beyond Women's Liberation

> *Liberation for women today means reaching across difficult boundaries that so often separate us as a human community— between Muslim, Christian, and Jew; industrialist and environmentalist; the powerful and the disenfranchised—and standing together for a world of justice and peace on behalf of our children and our grandchildren.* —JUANITA BROWN, *WHAT IS ENLIGHTENMENT?* MAGAZINE

Aside from being leaders each in their own way, most of these seven women are also mothers of adult children, daughters of aging parents, and wives, weaving their various roles into the tapestry of their lives. For women of our generation entering this century, it has not been easy to keep holding together the daily strands of our multiple roles and responsibilities. We have been at once devoted to our loved ones while also being drawn to or involved in large and expansive endeavors.

Many women in their forties or fifties are still loving and parenting children or teenagers while they also feel this evolutionary shift occurring among us. As the author and president of Foundation for Conscious Evolution, Barbara Marx Hubbard says, as quoted in *What Is Enlightenment?* magazine, "We are shifting our passion for maximum procreation to co-creation ... a yearning to give birth to our greater self and to a world that is viable, sustainable and compassionate." While we contribute in co-creation, many of us have developed new levels of confidence and self-authority founded in transparency and humility. Yet, in the midst of this, interspersed with a range of intense emotions from the darkness of sadness, to anger, into the light of love, joy and gratitude, we have also had moments of feeling overwhelmed. And it remains challenging for most of us to care deeply for ourselves and our well-being when we also strive to infuse our passion and excellence into all that we do.

While we in the West are enjoying the rights and freedoms we now take for granted, as Margaret Wheatley reminds us, large economic and social inequities remain among men and women worldwide. These inequities are now being addressed by countless charitable organizations, foundations and individuals such as the ones you have read about in this book. As middle-class Western women's basic survival needs have been virtually assured, we have moved toward other needs on the Maslow model of development. Hence, we are increasingly bringing forward our self-actualized potential to be of service to others. When we help and support communities and women across the world, particularly, we hold many hopes in our heart; two of mine are that everyone will have access to educational opportunities that can lift them out of poverty and that no mother should ever suffer the atrocious pain of seeing her child die of starvation.

Women's philanthropy

*My general ethical understanding of what it would mean
to be liberated is to not be dominated by one's own tendencies
toward narcissism so that we are free to care, to recognize the
equality of others, and to care about them as equals.*
—MARTHA NUSSBAUM, *WHAT IS ENLIGHTENMENT?* MAGAZINE

According to recent research, a majority of educated women in North America are "free to care," as demonstrated by their concerns for the welfare of others expressed through philanthropy. Some major studies are still in process, but the following recent research results from the Center on Philanthropy at Indiana University were published in the June 2008 special philanthropy issue of *Town & Country* magazine:

- Single women are much more likely than single men to make philanthropic gifts.
- Married women generally influence their husbands to contribute more.
- Among affluent married couples, women steer the household toward donating to education.

Town & Country conducted its own survey of nearly 2,000 American women, 30.5 percent of whom were between the ages of 45 and 54. Standing out from the published survey results, when women were asked, "How important is it to you to support causes that relate especially to women?" 41 percent said it was somewhat important and 40 percent said it was very important. When women were asked, "In what ways have you contributed to charitable groups in the past three years?" the responses revealed that many women contributed in more ways than one, which resulted in these findings:

- 89% by donating money
- 80% by donating goods and services
- 70% by volunteering
- 49% by raising money
- 49% by serving on a committee or board

One of the conclusions *Town & Country* reached from this survey is that "women give from the heart, men from their pocketbook."

In their book *The Transformational Power of Women's Philanthropy*, authors Sondra Shaw-Hardy and Martha Taylor affirm that there has been a huge growth in women's philanthropy over the past fifteen years. These authors identify several motives underlying the giving by women: a desire to connect to causes they care about and see the human face of their impact, to celebrate the fun of giving, and to take risks to transform society rather than maintain the status quo.

When it comes to volunteering, a myth still lingers that some women volunteer out of boredom or because they want something to occupy their days. But Lynn Korda Kroll, president of Women's Philanthropy of UJA–Federation of New York, acknowledges that things have changed. She was quoted in this special issue of *Town & Country* as having said: "Women require a higher level of stimulation and satisfaction than they used to get from volunteer work or social opportunities. They're working to make the world better." Indeed, at this pivotal point in time, more and more women *and* men want to transcend their differences and make a difference together. The time has come for us all to stand, across genders and generations, on behalf of the Future we dream of.

The next, final chapter intends to spark further insights in you while you clarify or reaffirm your purpose, "lead" your legacy, and give of yourself close to home or far afield on our beloved Earth.

Questions to ponder

- How does your way of contributing, to the welfare of others or to the preservation of nature, resemble or contrast with the work of the seven women profiled in this chapter?
- What would need to change in your circumstances or your attitude for you to feel even more "free to care" about others as equal?
- If you are a woman who has felt pulled in different directions from different roles and impulses, what are they? How are you choosing to respond to these inner and outer pressures?
- Where in the world, including your own community, are you most drawn to invest yourself or your resources in benevolent endeavors?

CHAPTER 14

Living Your Mission, Leaving Your Legacy

I discovered that people are not really afraid of dying;
they're afraid of not ever having lived, not ever having
deeply considered their life's higher purpose,
not ever having stepped into that purpose and
at least tried to make a difference.

—Joseph Jarowski

B y the time we enter our fifties or sixties, most of us have gained an appreciation of the ephemeral nature of life. With this realization, the urge to use our remaining years in the most meaningful and enjoyable way possible intensifies. And as I have heard it said, "When you die, the only thing you get to take with you is what you've given away to others."

This chapter brings further to light the great sense of responsibility you might feel, as I do, recognizing that we have been entrusted with the gift of life. Out of that recognition can be born a joyful sense of mission. Here you will find an integrative summary that elaborates on the developmental opportunities of midlife. This chapter also presents eight types of practices that are reflective of life-affirming values and conducive to fulfillment in midlife and eldership in the twenty-first century. Consider these touch-stones as you forge your own path to fulfillment in the coming years.

Leading—not spending—your life

> *Life is not a brief candle, it is a brilliant torch that*
> *I want to make burn as brightly as possible before*
> *passing it on to the next generation.*
> — GEORGE BERNARD SHAW

Pondering the words of George Bernard Shaw, can you feel the urge to "make burn as brightly as possible" the brilliant torch you intend to pass on? We all know the common expression of *leaving a legacy*, which refers to being remembered for what we have passed on to others after we depart. Some people are unconcerned about this, preferring to live fully and trusting that after they die a positive influence will remain among their loved ones. Others do not want to be forgotten and hope that by the end of their life, they will feel satisfied from having reached their full potential and made a significant difference. If you are among the latter, I suggest you think of *leading* your legacy from a proactive and intentional mindset. This implies that you are mindful of using your character strengths, of living in congruence with your highest values, and of tapping the spirit of leadership to create a wondrous ripple effect with the rest of your life.

Those of us who have high expectations of ourselves may fear that our desire to make a significant difference is not fulfilled because we have not *done* enough. But contributions through actions, large or small, near or far, all have importance in the overall systemic functioning and betterment of our world. Consider, for example, how tiny organisms such as insects play their essential part in large, interrelated ecological systems. If bees were to completely disappear off the face of the Earth, we have been told, our continuity on the planet would be furthermore seriously threatened.

Sometimes we believe we have not *done* enough because we underestimate to what extent our way of *being* can have a positive impact on others. "Making a difference" is also about expressing your caring through simple moments in which you support, encourage or otherwise show your love toward others. Most of us never forget a person who is remarkably focused on possibilities and potential rather than obstacles and limitations. Around such a person, we often feel empowered and seen in our best light. Perhaps you too have come to realize that something particularly wise, kind or insightful you have said has been etched in someone's "heart memory."

Clearly, in the end, our legacy emanates from the strength and clarity of our life themes, the choices we made, the actions we have taken, and the way we have related to others throughout our life. If your life's message emphasizes the importance of embodying love, being fair and just, having integrity or displaying an indomitable spirit, you know that you will be remembered. And you may recall that Mother Teresa said we can only "do small things with a lot of love," and that is the essence of creating a significant legacy.

Albert Einstein reminded us of our interdependence and urged us to break out of the illusion that we are separate from others. I believe that becoming free of this illusion is part of the required curriculum while we are in the School of Life on Earth.

Life lessons from the other side

In the *Ode* magazine of December 2005, an interview with the cardiologist Pim Van Lommel conveyed this man's passion for discovering what life is really about through the accounts of some of his patients' near-death experiences (NDEs). After many years as a cardiologist, Van Lommel became so intensely intrigued by what he heard about such experiences that he founded the International Association for Near-Death Studies, a research institute.

In the *Ode* interview, Van Lommel explained that most people who have had an NDE describe it as magnificent, enriching their life and freeing them from the fear of death. Regardless of their religious or spiritual orientation, most people experience an insightful flashback of their life in the presence of a being made of light. This irrevocably changes people's understanding of what life is about, reorienting them to lead their life much more intentionally. Based on his research in this field, Van Lommel is now convinced that "every thought we have, positive or negative, has an impact on us, each other and nature." With this deeper understanding of life, those who experience an NDE adopt values based on their new realization that they are one with nature, others and the planet.

Sometimes it is in the aftermath of tragedy that we learn profound lessons that alter the course of our life. Such was the case for "Dr. Chandra," who overcame and transformed devastating adversity into a triumph of human spirit and generativity.

Leading and serving beyond adversity

Although we may have a vision for what we want to do in midlife and or retirement, sometimes our best plans are pre-empted by events we could never have imagined. As the years move us further into eldership, we are likely to experience adversity in the form of losses. In some cases, such loss occurs long before we could ever anticipate that possibility. This was the case for Chadrasekhar Sankurathri, PhD (Dr. Chandra), a successful scientist who immigrated to Canada from India with his wife in the 1970s.

In June of 1985, Dr. Chandra's wife Manjari and their two young children, Srikiran and Sarada, boarded a plane in Canada, headed to India for a vacation. The flight never made it past the coast of Ireland, because a bomb planted by terrorists exploded on board. After nearly four years of intense grief, Dr. Chandra transformed his pain into humanitarianism in action and founded the Manjari Sankurathri Memorial Foundation (www.msmf.ca). This foundation is dedicated to empowering the poor in India through quality education and heath services such as cataract surgery at the grassroots community level.

When I met Dr. Chandra in 2006 I was struck by his humble, quiet demeanor. He explained that his relentless humanitarian pursuits are fueled by his enduring love for his deceased family and his desire to keep honoring them through the foundation's benevolent mission. Indeed, his actions have been extraordinarily beneficial to communities in India. For example, in 1992, the foundation opened a school, which has enabled hundreds of young children to receive an excellent education, complimentary lunches, medical checkups and medicines. Additionally, since 1999 the number of cataract surgeries performed *per month* through the foundation's hospital in India has exceeded one thousand. Through his foundation, Dr. Chandra is leading a magnificent legacy.

Your legacy in the workplace

As you read this, you may be among those who are thriving at the peak of their potential in their fifties or early sixties. Or you may be currently experiencing degrees of dissatisfaction or frustration at work. If you are involved in a workplace that you expect to leave in a few years, you may be thinking about exercising your influence to effect positive changes. Linda Dunkel, president and CEO of Interaction Associates, whose work is described in the previous chapter, exemplified the courage to take bold new initiatives when she collaboratively funded and created the Interaction Institute for Social Change.

Those among us who have achieved our career aspirations and reached notable levels of expertise and credibility often feel freer to innovate. If you feel this way, chances are, you may want to nudge the status quo in some way and deliver your genius through new initiatives. In *One: The Art and Practice of Conscious Leadership*, author Lance Secretan writes about the CASTLE principles to guide leaders away from old paradigms and into a "higher ground" of integrity and authenticity. CASTLE is an acronym for six characteristics that describe what Secretan calls the Higher Ground Leader in organizations. These are Courage, Authenticity, Service, Truth, Love and Effectiveness. The impulses to embrace these values and ideals are within us, says Secretan. As the impulses come forward from within, they help to "guide the contribution of brilliance" among people in an organization.

Anita Roddick, founder of the Body Shop, was one entrepreneur and leader who loved to take a stand for what she believed in while conducting her business. In her book *Business as Unusual: My Entrepreneurial Journey, Profits with Principles*, the late Roddick writes in depth about "breaking the rules" and instigating worthwhile changes while following one's innermost principles and highest values. Such initiatives may be, for example, a program of corporate philanthropy, a new way of "greening" your organization or a program of wellness for employees.

Although sometimes instigated in order to remain effective and competitive, employee health programs are increasingly being adopted by employers. Between 1993 and 1999, there was a 20 percent increase in the number of Canadian companies that reported having an employee wellness program. Among these are companies such as Telus Corporate Health Services in Burnaby, British Columbia, which saved $4.5 million in 1998 after implementing an employee wellness program that included on-site yoga and meditation. Evidence reveals that besides cost benefits, such programs also have a positive impact on the organization as a whole.

Those who are in positions of leadership have more opportunity to engage others in new endeavors and wise actions that will have lasting impact. But *everyone* can positively affect their work culture: by fostering harmony through the way they communicate or by being a model of integrity even when others stray from "doing the right thing." Although most workplaces are complex systems impacted by numerous forces beyond our control, employees can still exert a positive influence through various simple initiatives. For example, instigating a personal check-in time at the start of a staff meeting can help to humanize the workplace, build trust, and infuse more caring in the organization. Paradoxically, when each person takes two to three minutes to share from their personal life and be acknowledged by others, they become more present to the professional tasks before them. Feeling a sense of congruence between who we are personally and what we do professionally is part of the inner dynamic of engagement whether at work or beyond the workplace.

Developing your mission

> *If your purpose is only about you, it has no branches.*
> *If it is only about the rest of the world, it has no roots.*
> — DAUNA MARKOVA

Developing a mindset that is conducive to gaining clarity about one's renewed purpose and mission is an important part of the transition of midlife and re-engagement. Some of my coaching clients who are approaching retirement initially have a perception of retirement as a time container soon to be empty of working hours. Their impulse is to fill up the hours with activities to keep busy. But as I stated previously, days replete with *time-filling* activities do not necessarily generate a balanced and *fulfilling* life.

During workshops or one-on-one work, I encourage some clients to adopt a different metaphor as an image that facilitates their life transition. I suggest they think of their life as a school in motion or a voyage and identify their last chosen destination (field of endeavor/occupation/purpose) and the vehicle (including practices and profession) they have used thus far. For example, a previous client, whom I will call William, had been an accountant for over thirty years whose main occupation was to "balance the books." His deeper purpose and satisfaction, he realized, came from also helping his clients to experience more financial security and gain from sound, lucrative investments. The vehicle he used for serving his purpose in this field was the practice of accountancy.

William originally came to me for help after having heard the unconfirmed statistic that if someone retires at age 65 with no sense of purpose or direction, they will only live an average of 3.6 more years. With my guidance, this client reevaluated his priorities and values, reawakened dormant interests and realized that he also needs time to explore new destinations. Together we developed an emerging vision that includes him continuing to advise a selected few clients on investments, volunteering to generate a sense of social utility, and initiating practices conducive to his wellness and to enhanced relationships with relatives and friends. Through his renewed sense of engagement William is no longer concerned about being at risk of premature death.

My friend Brigitte Rathje, who resides in Victoria, British Columbia, has been a devoted teacher (her vehicle) for several decades, supporting children to learn what they need to succeed in their education (her purpose and destination). But over the years, she realized that her deeper calling was to help children to grown and to "blossom in their full potential." Being a lifelong learner, Brigitte completed various training programs during her fifties, including certification as a clinical hypnotherapist, as a Dynamic Facilitation Skills trainer and as a self-esteem and personal development trainer with Jack Canfield, co-author of *Chicken Soup for the Soul*. "These opened a whole new world to me," she said, pointing out that she enjoyed delving into the power of the mind. While approaching the end of her career as a teacher in the public school system, Brigitte has been preparing to change her "vehicle" and head for new horizons.

Soon Brigitte will retire from her current workplace and devote herself to helping adults in midlife and eldership "keep contributing their full potential." Having developed numerous contacts and relationships as well as an entrepreneurial spirit, over the past decade, Brigitte is now well prepared to offer her knowledge and wisdom in new avenues of personal development. Through the workshops she will lead and the one-on-one guidance she will provide, Brigitte will use facilitation, leadership and counseling as vehicles to deliver her transformative work. She is a great example of someone tapping the potential of midlife to determine a new destination, develop a new vehicle, and gradually move toward a fulfilling and purposeful re-engagement.

For many of us the School of Life is not meant to be a smooth, steady climb on a straightforward road. Instead, the trajectory is often one of multiple meandering paths that tend to converge by the end of midlife. We typically go through various cycles on our developmental path, which naturally spirals upwards into the higher spiritual realizations. When we are true to our developmental path and embrace its opportunities, we are more likely to gain clarity about our purpose in the course of midlife or in the gateway of eldership. During these life stages, we can gain the perspective to see who we really are, grasp the underlying themes of our life, and truly possess all we have said and done. This serves to reaffirm our direction or help us to re-engage in a more authentic and congruent orientation and destination.

Ways of giving—including my story

I slept and dreamt that life was joy. I awoke and saw that life
was service. I acted and behold service was joy.
— RABINDRANATH TAGORE

The stories and examples you have read in this book illustrate the different ways of giving of yourself, of your resources and your love. Of course, there are many more ways of helping others or contributing to the preservation of our natural world; additional suggestions are listed particularly in the "Caring practices" and the "Sustainability practices" section on page 181.

These days so many of us are overwhelmed and nearly dying for a moment of peace and rest in the midst of our fast busy lives. If that is often how you feel, you may wonder how you can give when you feel empty and overly stressed much of the time. Let me remind you of the wise words of Brother David Steindl-Rast, who said, "The answer to exhaustion is not necessarily rest, it is wholeheartedness," Doing what we love wholeheartedly infuses more energy and joy into our life. For my part, I can emphatically say that helping others to realize their dreams is one of the most enjoyable, energizing and fulfilling pleasures of my life.

Now, some people are very methodical and logical in their approach to selecting a cause or an organization in which they want to get involved to give back. Others, such as myself, begin with a sincere heart-felt intention to give, knowing that this in itself invites opportunities to be of service, often by timely coincidences or synchronicity. Like others, I also like to use discernment in considering various opportunities that I may feel drawn to from time to time.

In the course of contributing our resources to some cause or organization, we may become aware that something about it is not satisfying. Perhaps we realize that too much of the money received by an organization goes to their administrative expenses. Or we want to support a philanthropic project being organized elsewhere in the world but later learn that the project encountered multiple obstacles and fell through. Some people bring their collective intelligence to bear in the process of deciding how to give back. For example, relatives, friends or colleagues can meet in philanthropic circles to explore possibilities of giving collaboratively.

It is beyond the scope of this book to provide detailed information about how, where, when and to whom you might give or how to get involved in a cause that calls you. Personally, I have volunteered, given to charities and served in various ways in my life thus far, but my first trip to Bali in 2004 opened new possibilities of helping that have turned out to be deeply satisfying.

As mentioned in the chapter on lifestyle choices, I went to Bali for the Quest for Global Healing conferences. You have read that I enjoy the Balinese culture for its emphasis on the interconnectedness of all beings and the relaxed pace of life, which is conducive to being centered in one's authentic self. I also appreciate the spiritual practices and ceremonies that keep the bonds strong between the Balinese people.

Driven by my love of people and my intense curiosity about how the Balinese live, I was keen to converse with the locals when I arrived in Ubud, Bali. Among the people I met, Sang Tu stood out as a young man, in his late twenties then, working in a shop for tourists near my hotel. Talking with him, I realized he was very knowledgeable about his culture and we enjoyed sharing insights about our respective societies. It was clear to me that he had a very caring heart and a deep hunger for intellectual stimulation and learning. While talking with him, I also heard about his dream to "go over-seas" and experience North America.

During my last evening in Bali, in conversation with Sang Tu, I asked him if he ever dreamed of going to university. "Of course," he replied. Then he explained that he was the youngest of eight children and that his father had saved some money for his children's higher education. But then, when Sang Tu was 18 years old, his father became ill, was hospitalized, and all of the savings were used up for medical care before he passed away. Not only was attending university no longer possible, but Sang Tu also had to work to help support his aging mother.

Following my return to Canada I continued to correspond with Sang Tu via e-mail, and our friendship grew. I then offered to pay for some courses that he would likely enjoy attending in his area. Sang Tu accepted my offer and with his love for languages, attended two courses in Russian that he felt would be useful because of the growing number of Russian tourists coming to Bali. Then Sang Tu began to work at the hotel I had stayed at and his income improved. After he took a driving course that I also sponsored, he was able to earn a little extra by taking tourists on sight-seeing tours.

When I returned to Bali in May 2006, I was jubilant to see him again and my other friend Plentung, whom I had barely gotten to know during my first visit. This time Sang Tu invited me to his family compound, where his mother cooked a meal for us. He showed me with great pride the lami-nated certificates of completion for the courses I had paid for. Then he gave me gifts for my children to express his gratitude. I recall saying, "That's al-most too much." He replied, "Don't be shy; these are just things. What you gave me will last my whole life." I was awed by the extent of his thankfulness.

In 2007 I decided to return to Bali to participate in the Awakening Global Action event. This time I thought I would give Sang Tu another, even better opportunity to learn and grow. Over several months, I took all of the steps required to sponsor Sang Tu to come back to Canada with me for a visit and an educational opportunity. Many phone conversations, e-mails and letters were needed for him to get his passport and visa, to coordinate our flights, and to sign up Sang Tu for a course at the University of British Columbia. At the same time, I fundraised about half of the necessary money for all of this, through the generosity of some friends and relatives.

While I was in Bali in 2007, I also enjoyed talking with my friend Plentung, who worked at the same hotel. One evening, in a lengthy conversation with him, I learned that his biggest dream was to make his father happy by paying for the education of Suardika, Plentung's younger brother. I recall being moved by this and telling him to hold his dream in his heart with all his might. The next day I shared this conversation with some American friends of mine who said, in response, "We can help." The result is that as I write this, the second year of university fees and expenses have been paid for Suardika, who is proud to be the first one to have this educational opportunity in his village. A recent e-mail from Plentung went straight to my heart. It said, "Without you [including my sponsoring friends], my father's dream could never have come true."

Back from Bali in August 2007, I hosted Sang Tu in Vancouver for one month while he attended a part-time English improvement course for foreign students. During his stay my children and I enjoyed exposing him to cultural events, to some of our nearby islands, to my favorite "hot spots" in the city and to natural areas of beauty such as the top of Whistler Mountain. There, he was gleeful as he touched snow for the first time in his life. At the top of that mountain, he seemed to feel literally elevated into his higher self, affirmed in his knowing that dreams can really come true when we believe in them.

Sang Tu had been married a few months before coming to Vancouver. Now he and his wife, Kadek, have a beautiful baby girl, whom I look forward to meeting when I return to Bali. Meanwhile, Sang Tu's life continues to expand and improve while he draws new opportunities to himself through his greater self-confidence, his broader perspectives, and his desire to excel in all that he does. And after having experienced our culture and glimpsed its challenges as well as its strengths, he has a new appreciation for the best of his culture: the strong family and community bonds and the spirituality and meaning that form the fabric of everyday life.

From Sang Tu I learned a few things about what is really important in life. Through the subtle influence of my friendship with him and my time in Bali, my way of prioritizing my values has shifted. For example, material things have much less importance, loving and seeing the best in others is more important, while living in integrity with my heart's desires is also paramount as never before. I also learned from the Balinese influence to better savor the moment and to avoid rushing through my life. One of these lessons was emphasized again during a walk I took with Sang Tu and my friend Karen in Vancouver. She and I started to walk quickly on the shoreline path in order to "get some exercise," but then Sang Tu remarked, "In Bali, we only walk fast if there is an emergency."

Through my story, I imagine you can grasp that this emerging experience of helping in Bali has brought me profound satisfaction. Now I want to keep helping others. I am in the process of developing a small nonprofit project to give more young people the opportunity to access higher education. And next time, a young woman will be chosen to have this chance. You may know that tourism has been one of the main economic streams of revenue in Bali. Given the ecological concerns about travel, and the rising cost of travel due to our depleting sources of oil, fewer tourists from North America are likely to go to Bali in the future. Hence the urgent need for more Balinese to have access to higher education, to develop new industries and possibilities for employment.

Certainly we must exercise caution when we find causes we want to support elsewhere in the world. We must be particularly careful to avoid imposing solutions that are not culturally practical or that overlook the traditions of the people we want to help. What is more, we need to make sure that our help is generative in nature, that it ultimately supports people to become more self-sufficient while they keep embracing the best of the culture to which they belong. Sometimes our impulse to help brings us into an ethical dilemma. There are no easy solutions to the complex and numerous challenges all around our planet. But let us remember that when we take collaborative actions with others to help and when we give with the appropriate attitudes and intentions, we are likely to make an invaluable and significant difference.

When we develop a right attitude of compassion
and gratitude, we take a giant step towards solving our
personal and international problems.
— HIS HOLINESS THE DALAI LAMA

Developmental opportunities that beckon us in midlife

The call to generativity illustrated through my story is but one of the developmental opportunities that present themselves in midlife. This section further explores these opportunities, also identified at the end of chapter 3. Although the shift toward these changes typically begins to occur in midlife, from the mid-forties onwards, you may recognize some aspects of this developmental growth in yourself right through your sixties. A list of practices that can optimize your development, helping you embrace your highest values and experience fulfillment, follows starting on page 179.

Reconnect with and listen to our authentic self.
This process, which can be life-long, was explored particularly in chapters 3 and 5. Beyond the roles we have embraced in our personal and professional life, our authentic self, the Source of life energy within, yearns to come to the fore and take the lead in midlife. In the process of connecting with the awareness at the core of our being, we can better hear the small voice within. With this inner guidance we are moved to live authentically, speak and act in accordance with our truth and heal any incongruence between who we are and what we do. The more we trust and listen to that small voice within, the more it makes itself clear to us and guide us in our choices, our intentions, our communications and our actions.

Slow down enough to enjoy life because we are more aware of its preciousness and its precariousness.
Navigating the middle passage, we are called to apportion our time and energies according to what is most meaningful and important in our life right now, because we do not know when it will end. Hence, we are wise to treat our life as precious while we practice—through mindfulness—the art of savoring and making the most of every moment even in the midst of countless responsibilities and preoccupations.

Express ourselves: free our voices and our creativity.
Every one of us has a deep desire to be seen and heard. Now more than ever, it is time for us to express ourselves, show up, lead and give our love, our joy, our insights and our wisdom through what we create, say, write or do. We

need to free ourselves from our inner critic and unleash our creative genius for others to be inspired by us and receive our gifts. Quite simply, everything we do can be done creatively.

Reassess our purpose and re-align our values with integrity.
As stated in various ways throughout this book, our values change through our developmental stages and it is important for us to recognize this natural evolution. In the course of re-identifying our strengths, our passions, and our purpose, we can redefine and re-order our priorities. Then we may better embody what we value most and shift our life accordingly.This does not necessarily involve changing our work, moving elsewhere or initiating a divorce. Sometimes the best change is to be made in our own mind, in our attitude or perspectives. (If you would like tools to help you gain clarity about your values, you may access a values assessment tool on my website: www.inspiredmomentum.com).

Connect more deeply with those we love and develop new relationships that enable us to see ourselves in a new light.
Connecting more deeply with others requires us to be present in mind and heart when interacting with others. If it is evident that your relationship with your significant other has deteriorated beyond possibilities of renewal or that you have grown apart, the time may come to consider changes. When we develop new friendships and relationships reflective of our authentic self, we can enjoy seeing ourselves in a fresh light in the eyes of a new friend or partner. Providing we remain fully present and communicate sincerely and skillfully, such relationships can affirm our growth, support our purpose, and provide the joyfulness of communion with another and with life itself.

Simplify our life so that less energy goes into acquiring and maintaining material things as their importance diminishes.
As explained in the chapter on lifestyle choices, simplifying our life often brings what is most important into sharper focus. Simplicity in our homes and lifestyles tends to invite a flow of energy and goodness to circulate through our life. The more we grow our inner wealth through our character strengths and actions, the less importance we place on our outer material things. Moreover, reducing our consumption through voluntary simplicity is an important part of developing sustainable ways of living.

Harness the spirit of generativity as a wind in our sails while we set out to make a difference in the lives of others.

Tapping our impulses to be of service and to help restore our harmony with nature are among the needs of our generation, which coincide with the multiple urgent needs all over the world. Our vitality is enhanced when we wholeheartedly engage in activities that provide a sense of social utility. Each one of us can create greater meaning and fulfillment in our life by following the inner guidance of our heart to give back, in some ways, and help to bring about the Future we long for.

Seven practices toward fulfillment

As we navigate these sometimes challenging developmental opportunities in midlife or while entering eldership, certain practices can sustain us and enrich our lives. Here are seven suggested types of practices that may help to ease your transition to eldership while also promoting generativity and fulfillment. While being conducive to your wellness, they also support the preservation of our planet. Several of the practices mentioned here are holistic in nature and defy categorization. For example, yoga can be both a wellness and spiritual practice. You probably are already practicing many of these values-in-action. Yet some of the practices may trigger your curiosity, help you recognize an impulse in yourself, or remind you of an intention you had about integrating them into your lifestyle.

Among these practices, some are expressions of the lifelong process of embodying our highest values and ideals, such as truth, beauty, excellence, honor and justice. Examples and a brief explanation are provided for each type of practice, but the brevity of the description is not to be interpreted as an oversimplification of the process of integrating these into daily living. Note that these activities and attitudes are meant to be practiced in a spirit of wisdom and equilibrium, to generate a balance between your inner and outer needs.

Contemplative and spiritual practices: meditating, yoga, enjoying the beauty of nature, reading poetry, being mindful, praying, practicing rituals and ceremonies.

Particularly in times of stress or worry, mindfulness practices can help soothe our nervous system and generate inner states of safety and calmness. This can be as simple as finding quiet time to sit alone and return your attention to your body and your breath. Allowing your fears to come up and be released as you relax your body and enable your worries to dissipate, you can learn to be more present and experience the safety in your present reality. In moments of feeling confused or unclear about what to do next, you may return your attention to your breath and ask yourself what you are feeling and needing in that moment. The more we heed our inner guidance, the more we feel at peace with ourselves; knowing that we are in the "right" place at the "right" time while doing and being what we are really meant to do and be. Mindfulness also helps us to refrain from allowing ourselves to be caught up in the techno-tyranny that holds many of us captive these days.

Contemplative practices are conducive to gratitude; by bringing our attention to what we are grateful for we can improve our relationships and enrich the quality and meaning in our life. Every time you remind yourself that you are, indeed, blessed—even in those times when you do not see or feel the blessings—you are figuratively lighting a candle in your world. In gratitude, you feel lighter, freer and happier. And the better you feel, the better those around you feel.

Wellness practices: doing yoga, eating a nutritious and balanced diet, maintaining good sleep habits, engaging in brain-stimulating activities, keeping active through various forms of movement, recreation or sport, such as walking, dancing, cycling, and so on.

These practices remind us of the importance of not taking our health for granted, and that we need to proactively care for ourselves in order to preserve or increase our well-being. When we treat our body as a temple, we are more likely to be appropriately discerning about the quality and the quantity of food we consume. Countless practices such as yoga or tai chi are conducive to body-mind-spirit wellness and therefore provide multiple benefits at once.

Creative practices: writing, poetry, singing, playing music, cooking, innovating, inventing, arts and crafts, expressing yourself in all you do.

The creative impulse is an inner dynamic that naturally thrives in us when we are happy, at peace and living with integrity. If your creative impulse has been dormant, you will bring it to life in the course of reconnecting with your authentic self and shaping your life accordingly. Even just the intention to do everyday things differently can spark more creativity. As well, allow yourself to invite and play with the creative Muse by trying new forms of expression—crafts, art or creative writing. When we tap this quality of energy within, we connect with the life force in us, and doing so keeps us feeling fully alive and even youthful.

Relationship practices: sharing, supporting, conversing, community-making through circles and various forms of group dialogue, leading, mentoring, nurturing intimacy and closeness with loved ones, communicating openly and sincerely, and so on.

At this time when the majority of our interactions occur through the phone or via e-mail, we need to make time for direct, human contact to nurture our friendships and relationships. Remaining in community with others is essential to keeping ourselves alive individually and collectively. Quite simply, our relationships provide essential meaning to our life, prevent us from becoming alienated from others and even help us to maintain our vitality. Moreover, our relationships help us to keep our hearts open which is essential to our continuity on Earth. As the eco-philosopher Joanna Macy said, "The closing of our hearts and minds is an even greater threat than global warming."

Caring practices: embodying altruism in action, tapping generativity within, serving, giving, volunteering, undertaking philanthropic and humanistic endeavors of various types, providing support.

You have read many examples of different ways of giving and caring throughout this book. As previously stated, it is important that you follow the inner guidance of your heart as you consider engaging in various caring practices. You may also wish to seek information through friends, websites and other sources before deciding when and if you are to get involved in a particular cause. It is important to make a difference in a way that works best for you, according to your inner and outer resources. And remember that even just a sincere, loving smile and caring words offered at a particular time can make a difference in someone's life.

Sustainability practices: recycling, purchasing fair-trade and organic products, minimizing your energy consumption, social and environmentally responsible investments, developing habits that reduce your ecological footprint and support the preservation of the natural world.

Countless organizations now offer information about what we can do to modify our lifestyle in order to live in a sustainable way. Some of these organizations are listed in the resources section. Living sustainably is our generational responsibility during this critical period on our planet. While we rise to the challenges, as overwhelming as they are, and make important changes, we can feel more at peace with ourselves knowing that we are doing our part for the future of our children and for the generations to come.

Moral excellence practices: displaying character strengths such as responsibility, "doing the right thing"—without righteousness, humility, compassion, fairness, forgiveness, courage, dignity, honor, respect, truthfulness, patience, equanimity, joy, and so on.

These are attitudes as well as virtues and character strengths that we can practice to feel more serene and to give our best as our gift to the world. During the wisdom years particularly, we can contribute equanimity as a counterweight to the reactivity that characterizes our present fear-driven culture. A concept often used in Buddhist philosophy, equanimity is a quality of energy that fosters temperance and a wisdom that can serve to inform our actions and intentions. This inner dynamic also helps us to embrace the difficult moments of life without being disrupted from our connectedness with the core of our being. Whether we are in midlife or early retirement, equanimity helps us to be anchored by our most honorable values and character strengths when facing challenges or adversity.

A few last words . . .

As you live forward from here on, may you see midlife and beyond as a source of fresh new beginnings. This freshness can arise "in the moment," each time you choose to create something new or respond differently to a recurring situation. The spirit of renewal is further infused in your life when you tap wholeheartedly the opportunities you discover in the course of your personal evolution. And your vitality is enhanced when you embrace, in your own way, the practices that bring into daily reality the values and ideals you cherish: excellence, beauty, love, justice, truth, peace, community, and generativity, to name a few.

Remember that whether you are committed to improving your health, overcoming adversity at work or taking on a philanthropic project, your focused intention and sincere engagement will help you achieve what you desire. And when you are purposefully engaged in a relationship, a project or an endeavor that is close to your heart, you do *live forward* because of the inspired momentum generated by the flow of love circulating through you.

As a generation, in this century, we now see that the future over the horizon is different than the one we dreamed of in the sixties or seventies. Most of us have grown in maturity, compassion and appreciation for the many paradoxes and dilemmas in our present culture and in our world. Grasping the sobering reality that the resources of the Earth are *finite*, we know that the next decades will be replete with challenges. But what is *not finite* is the resourcefulness and resilience of the human spirit that is the essence of who we are. And what is *not finite* is the extraordinary, creative power of our mind when used in loving synergy with the leading power of our heart. This is the miraculous, *infinite* power that has enabled, for example, a mother to lift a car to save her child. Each one of us can access more of this infinite resourcefulness as we keep lifting ourselves into the realm of consciousness where all possibilities exist.

More and more, in spite of our present social, economic and global ecological crises, we must hold our vision of a new world and harness these inner resources to weather the tumultuous sea ahead. In the spirit of humility, we can feel empowered by the visionary leaders of our past as we listen inward and to one another for answers to the difficult questions of our times. Let us rise to the honor of being the ancestors of the Future; let us do so for the sake of the beauty and innocence of our children, for the preservation of hope in the eyes of *their* children, for the precious magnificence of the natural world, and for every one of us now and into the Future.

REFERENCES AND RESOURCES

■ REFERENCES

Blanton, Brad. *Practicing Radical Honesty: How to Complete the Past, Live in the Present and Build a Future.* Sparrowhawk Publications, 2002.

Bohm, David. *Wholeness and the Implicate Order.* New York: Routledge, 2002.

Boyd, David R. *Sustainability within a Generation: A New Plan for Canada.* Vancouver, B.C.: David Suzuki Foundation, 2004. www.davidsuzuki.org/files/WOL/DSF-GG-En-Final.pdf

Bridges, William. *The Way of Transition: Embracing Life's Most Difficult Moments.* New York: Perseus Publishing, 2001.

Childre, Doc, and Deborah Rozman. *Transforming Anger: The HearthMath Solution for Letting Go of Rage, Frustration and Irritation.* Oakland, CA: New Harbinger Publications, 2003.

Church, Dawson. *The Genie in Your Genes: Epigenetic Medicine and the New Biology of Intention.* Fulton, CA: Elite Books, 2007.

Cohen, Gene. "The Myth of the Midlife Crisis." *Newsweek*, January 16, 2006.

Dass, Ram, and Paul Gorman. *How Can I Help? Stories and Reflection on Service.* New York: Knopf, 1985.

Edelman, Marian Wright. "A Time Forum: What if He Were Alive Today?" *Time*, January 9, 2006.

Erikson, Erik H. *Identity and the Life Cycle.* New York: W.W. Norton & Company, 1994.

———. *The Life Cycle Completed.* New York: W.W. Norton & Company, 1998.

Erikson, Erik H., Joan M. Erikson, and Helen Q. Kivnick. *Vital Involvement in Old Age.* New York: W.W. Norton & Company, 1994.

Frankl, Viktor E. *Man's Search for Meaning.* Boston: Beacon Press, 2006.

Fritz, Robert. *Creating: A Practical Guide to the Creative Process and How to Use It to Create Anything—a Work of Art, a Relationship, a Career or a Better Life.* New York: Ballantine Books, 1993.

———. *The Path of Least Resistance: Learning to Become the Creative Force in Your Own Life.* New York: Ballantine Books, 1989.

Gilbert, Elizabeth. *Eat, Pray, Love: One Woman's Search for Everything across Italy, India and Indonesia.* New York: Penguin, 2007.

Hagelin, John. "The Power of the Collective." *Shift*, June-August 2007.

Hawken, Paul. *Blessed Unrest: How the Largest Movement in the World Came into Being and Why No One Saw It Coming*. New York: Viking, 2007.

Hollis, James. *The Middle Passage: From Misery to Meaning in Midlife*. Studies in Jungian Psychology by Jungian Analysts. Toronto: Inner City Books, 1993.

Honoré, Carl. *In Praise of Slowness: Challenging the Cult of Speed*. New York: HarperCollins, 2005.

Johnson, Charles R. "The King We Need: Teachings for a Nation in Search of Itself." *Shambhala Sun*, January 2005. www.shambhalasun.com/index.php?option= content&task=view&id=1329&Itemid=247.

Johnson, Richard. *The New Retirement: The Ultimate Guide to the Rest of Your Life*. Rev. ed. New York: Rodale Books, 2007.

Kabat-Zinn, Jon. "How to Put Time on Your Side." *Ode*, May 2007. www.odemaga zine.com/doc/43/how_to_put_time_on_your_side/.

Kanner, Allen D., and Mary E. Gomes. "The All-Consuming Self." In *Ecopsychology: Restoring the Earth, Healing the Mind*, edited by Theodore Roszak, Allen D. Kanner, and Mary E. Gomes, 77–91. San Francisco: Sierra Club Books, 1995.

Kerry, John, and Teresa Heinz Kerry. *This Moment on Earth: Today's New Environmentalists and Their Vision for the Future*. PublicAffairs, 2007.

Kessel, Brent. *It's Not About the Money: Unlock your Money Type to Achieve Spiritual and Financial Abundance*. New York: HarperCollins, 2008.

Khalsa, Dharma Singh, MD, and Cameron Stauth. *Meditation as Medicine: Activate the Power of Your Natural Healing Force*. New York: Simon & Schuster, 2002.

King, Ruth. *Healing Rage: Women Making Inner Peace Possible*. Reprint ed., New York: Gotham, 2008.

Korstrom, Glen. "21st Century Retirees Ripe for Entrepreneurialism Indulgence." *Business in Vancouver*, August 22–28, 2006, p. 13.

Laucius, Joanne. "The Natural Way to Happiness." *Vancouver Sun*, May 3, 2008, pp. D1, D2.

Leider, Richard J., and David A. Shapiro. *Claiming Your Place at the Fire: Living the Second Half of Your Life on Purpose*. San Francisco: Berrett-Koehler Publishers, 2004.

Lindbergh, Anne Morrow. *Gift from the Sea*. New York: Pantheon Books, 1975.

Lipton, Bruce H. *The Biology of Belief: Unleashing the Power of Consciousness, Matter and Miracles*. Santa Rosa, CA: Elite Books, 2005.

Loehr, Jim, and Tony Schwartz. *The Power of Full Engagement: Managing Energy, Not Time, Is the Key to High Performance and Personal Renewal*. New York: Free Press, a division of Simon & Schuster, 2004.

McGregor, Karen. *Sculpting the Business Body: Strategies and Stories from Top Entrepreneurs*. Langley, B.C.: Behm Publishing, 2007.

Meade, Michael. *The World Behind the World*. Greenfire Press, 2008.

Merton, Thomas. Quoted by Charlie Badenhop in the Seishindo newsletter *Pure Heart, Simple Mind* 5, no. 6 (March 15, 2007). www.seishindo.org/newsletter/2007/06-value-of-suffering.html.

Moore, Thomas. *Care of the Soul: A Guide for Cultivating Depth and Sacredness in Everyday Life*. New York: Perennial, 1994.

O'Donohue, John. *Anam Cara: A Book of Celtic Wisdom*. New York: Cliff Street Books, 1997.

———. *Beauty: The Invisible Embrace*. New York: HarperCollins, 2004.

Pagels, Elaine. *The Gnostic Gospels*. New York: Random House, 2004.

Palmer, Parker. *A Hidden Wholeness: The Journey Toward an Undivided Life*. San Francisco: Jossey-Bass, 2004.

Pink, Daniel. *A Whole New Mind: Why Right-Brainers Will Rule the Future*. Rev. ed. New York: Riverhead Books, 2006.

Post, Stephen, and Jill Neimark. *Why Good Things Happen to Good People: The Exciting New Research that Proves the Link between Doing Good and Living a Longer, Healthier, Happier Life*. New York: Broadway Books, 2007.

Ram Dass. *Still Here: Embracing Aging, Changing, and Dying*. Edited by Mark Matousek and Marlene Roeder. New York: Riverhead Books, 2000.

Roddick, Anita. *Business as Unusual: My Entrepreneurial Journey, Profits with Principles*. West Sussex, U.K.: Anita Roddick Books, 2005.

St-Jean, Isabelle, and Dawson Church, eds. *Einstein's Business: Engaging Soul, Imagination and Excellence in the Workplace*. Santa Rosa, CA: Elite Books, 2007.

Secretan, Lance. *One: The Art and Practice of Conscious Leadership*. Caledon, ON: Secretan Center, 2006.

Senge, Peter. "A World Shaped by Choice." In *Living the Questions: Essays Inspired by the Work and Life of Parker J. Palmer*, edited by Sam M. Intrator, 322–30. San Francisco: Jossey-Bass, 2005.

Senge, Peter, Richard Ross, Bryan Smith, Charlotte Roberts, and Art Kleiner. *The Fifth Discipline Fieldbook: Strategies and Tools for Building a Learning Organization*. London: Nicholas Brealey Publishing, 1994.

Servan-Schreiber, David. "Be True to Your Cells." *Ode*, December 2007. www.odemagazine.com/doc/49/be-true-to-your-cells/.

Shaw-Hardy, Sondra, and Martha Taylor. *The Transformational Power of Women's Philanthropy: New Directions for Philanthropic Fundraising*. San Francisco: Jossey-Bass, 2006.

Shealy, Dr. Norman, and Dawson Church. *Soul Medicine: Awakening Your Inner Blueprint for Abundant Health and Energy*. 2nd ed. Fulton, CA: Energy Psychology Press, 2008.

Siegel, Bernie S. *Love, Medicine and Miracles: Lessons Learned about Self-Healing from a Surgeon's Experience with Exceptional Patients*. New York: Harper Paperbacks, 1990.

Tolle, Eckhart. *A New Earth: Awakening to Your Life's Purpose*. New York: Penguin, 2008.

———. *The Power of Now: A Guide to Spiritual Enlightenment*. Novato, CA: New World Library, 2004.

Town & Country magazine. Special philanthropy issue, June 2008.

Tourtellot, Jonathan. *National Geographic Traveler* [quoted in chap. 9; *Ode*]

Tutu, Desmond. *No Future without Forgiveness*. New York: Doubleday, 2000.

Twist, Lynne. *The Soul of Money: Transforming Your Relationship with Money and Life*. New York: W.W. Norton & Company, 2003.

Wheatley, Margaret J. *Finding Our Way: Leadership for an Uncertain Time*. San Francisco: Berrett-Koehler Publishers, 2007.

Whyte, David. *Crossing the Unknown Sea: Work as a Pilgrimage of Identity*. New York: Riverhead Books, 2001.

———. *The Heart Aroused: Poetry and the Preservation of the Soul in Corporate America*. New York: Doubleday Business, 1996.

Williamson, Marianne. *The Age of Miracles: Embracing the New Midlife*. Carlsbad, CA: Hay House, 2008.

■ RESOURCES

ACCESS (African Canadian Continuing Education Society). www.acceskenya.org.
Founded by George and Beth Scott, ACCES helps young Africans obtain the skills and education needed to benefit themselves and their society.

Avaaz.org, the World in Action www.avaaz.org
This is a global web movement whose mission statement is: To close the gap between the world we have, and the world most people everywhere want.

Bali Institute for Global Renewal www.baliinstitute.org
Founded by Maria Jaffe, the Bali Institute offers education, training and leadership programs that inspire people to enact individual and collective initiatives that make a difference.

Be the Change Earth Alliance www.bethechangecircles.org
The mission of Be The Change Earth Alliance, directed by Maureen Jack-Lacroix, is to create a community of people willing to support each other to be the change required for an environmentally sustainable, spiritually fulfilling and socially just human presence on Earth.

Berkana Institute www.berkana.org
Co-founded by Margaret Wheatley, this institute connects and supports pioneering, life-affirming leaders around the world who strengthen their community by working with the wisdom and wealth already present in its people, traditions and environment.

Breakthroughs Unlimited Inc. www.breakthroughsunlimited.com
Myriam Laberge is the co-founder of Breakthroughs Unlimited whose mission is to help organizations achieve their noble goals through the power of vision, dialogue, participation and leadership.

Bridges, Branches & Braids www.healingrage.com
Ruth King's website outlining the products and services she provides to help people to understand and transform rage, and support the discharge of trauma that gives birth to rage.

Builders Without Borders www.builderswithoutborders.com
Founded by Neil Griggs, BWB is an international network of ecological builders who advocate the use of natural, local, and affordable materials in construction. BWB creates educational materials and opportunities to empower communities, organizations and owner-builders.

Center for Courage & Renewal (CCR) www.couragerenewal.org
This center, founded by Parker J. Palmer, is an educational non-profit organization that strengthens individuals, professions, and communities through retreats and programs that help people reconnect who they are with what they do.

Clown One Italia www.patchadams.org
Associates of Patch Adams, Ginevra Sanguigno and Italo Bertolasi lead clowning tours in Italy. The goal of these tours is to bring love, compassion, fun and the spirit of peace and friendship everywhere for everyone.

Community Friends www.communityfriends.org
Carsten Henningsen is the founding director of this non-profit organization dedicated to making high-impact investments in social businesses, micro-entrepreneurships, village collectives and community-wide enterprises, the return for which is measured in financial, social and environmental returns.

Cultural Creatives www.culturalcreatives.org
This website provides information about the Cultural Creatives and features the book: *The Cultural Creatives: How 50 Million People Are Changing the World*, by Paul H.Ray, PhD and Sherry Ruth Anderson PhD.

For The GrandChildren – Being Present for the Future www.4tgc.org
This organization, founded by Rich Henry and Victor Bremson, produces Inter-generational-Intercultural Dialogues and events for groups and individuals to help bring about a more environmentally sustainable, spiritually fulfilling and socially just human presence on Earth.

Foundation for Conscious Evolution www.evolve.org
Founded by Barbara Marx Hubbard, this site includes a newsletter and outlines inspiring and educational programs that support the conscious evolution of humanity.

Global Footprint Network www.footprintnetwork.org
This organization's mission is to support a sustainable economy by advancing the Ecological Footprint, a measurement tool that makes the reality of planetary limits relevant to decision-makers throughout the world.

Greenopolis.com www.greenopolis.com
Greenopolis.com is the first "green," interactive, collaborative, educational website to bring together communities, environmental organizations, universities, foundations and corporations to reward individuals for making incremental positive environmental changes.

HeartMath www.heartmath.com
This organization is internationally recognized for being dedicated to facilitating heart-based living—people relying on the intelligence of their heart in concert with their minds to improve health, performance, relationships and well-being at home and in the workplace.

Interaction Associates www.interactionassociates.com
President and CEO Linda Dunkel collaboratively leads this company, which helps clients solve business problems, drawing on nearly 40 years of innovation in the people-and-performance side of business.

Kyosei Consulting International, Inc. www.kyoseiconsulting.com
Andrea Jacques is the CEO of this company which is a human resources training, development, and consulting firm dedicated to creating a new vision of work.

Manjari Sankurathri Memorial Foundation www.msmf.ca
Founded by Dr. Chandra Sankurathri, this foundation promotes rural community development through education, health care and disaster relief programs.

Meetup.com www.meetup.com
Meetup is the world's largest network of local groups making it easy for anyone to organize a local group or find one of the thousands already meeting face-to-face.

Mindfulness Meditation CDs and Tapes wwwmindfulnesscds.com
The site offers mindfulness CDs and information about programs, retreats and workshops lead by Dr. Jon Kabat-Zinn, an internationally known meditation teacher, author, researcher, and clinician in the fields of mind/body medicine, integrative medicine, lifestyle change, and self-healing.

Pachamama Alliance www.pachamama.org
Co-founded by Lynne Twist, the Pachamama Alliance's mission is two-fold: To preserve the Earth's tropical rainforests by empowering the indigenous people who are its natural custodians; to contribute to the creation of a new global vision of equity and sustainability for all.

Portfolio21 www.portfolio21.com
Carsten Henningsen is the chairmen of this company, which has been a pioneer in the field of social and environmental investing since 1982.

Quest for Global Healing www.questforglobalhealing.org
This site features information about the Bali conferences organized and produced by Marcia Jaffe and her team in 2004 and 2006.

Society for Organizational Learning www.solonline.org
Founded by Peter Senge, SOL's purpose is to discover (research), integrate (capacity development) and implement (practice) theories and practices of organizational learning for the interdependent development of people and their institutions and communities.

Soul of Money Institute www.soulofmoney.org
Lynne Twist founded this institute which is a center for exploring and sharing the best practices, theories, and attitudes that enable people to relate to money and the money culture with greater freedom, power and effectiveness.

Sound Essence Project www.soundessenceproject.org
Susan Bradbury developed this non-profit corporation with the intention to create a cross-cultural network of resources in an environment of mutual learning with an emphasis on cultural sustainability.

Turn Your Face to the Sun Travel www.turnyourfacetothesun.com
Founded by Nancy Klinkhamer, this company offers stimulating and spiritual travel experiences that combine activity, interaction with local cultures and viewing awe-inspiring sacred sites.

US Partnership for Education for Sustainable Development
www.uspartnership.org
This site includesThe Inspired Futures Campaign, a national initiative lead by Douglas Cohen to make available to youth (15 to 30 years old) programs of leadership development and inter-generational mentoring.

Walking Together for Health and Development www.caminamosjuntos.org
This site features the work of Susan Smith and her team who are devoted to fostering self-sufficiency and rebuilding community in Tlamacazapa, Mexico.

Wildly Free Woman www.wildlyfreewoman.com
Developed by Gaye Abbott, WildyFreeWoman is a website dedicated to the luxuriant growth and embodied confident expression of all women everywhere, assisting women 50+ to lead a heart and soul satisfying life!

World Center of Compassion for Children International www.wccci.org
Betty Williams is the founder of this organization. Its mission is to create a strong political voice for children in areas of stress due to war, hunger or social, economic, or political upheaval and to respond to their expressed needs materially and emotionally.